The Children's Menu

Bite Size Lessons on the Gospel Message
For Children and Their Families

Based on Scripture,
Following the Seasons of the Christian Worship Year, and
Indexed to Lectionary Readings of the Bible

Wesley Joseph Mills

Quiet Waters Publications
Bolivar, Missouri
2010

For information contact:
Quiet Waters Publications
P.O. Box 34, Bolivar MO 65613-0034.
E-mail: QWP@usa.net.
For prices and order information visit:
http://www.quietwaterspub.com

Cover design: Mike Lee, Digital Media Faculty,
York County Community College

ISBN 978-1-931475-49-5
Library of Congress Control Number: 2010936430

Presented in gratitude for my children—Matthew, Danielle, and Jesse—and offered in memory of my grandfathers, Florian Lester Clark and Albert Douglass Mills, whose lives were often given in loving service to children and youth

CONTENTS

PREFACE

Numerous Scripture texts and themes come to mind in undertaking to compile a book of children's meditations. Each in its own way contributes a thread to the tapestry of thought that comprises an anthology of messages such as this.

Surely, the admonition of Jesus comes to mind: "Let the little children come to me; do not stop them; for it is to such as these that the kingdom of God belongs. Truly I tell you, whoever does not receive the kingdom of God as a little child will never enter it" (Mark 10:14-15). Indeed, a word of affirmation of children is central to preparation of messages for them.

Also, the rhetorical postulate from the Apostle Paul may come to mind: "The same Lord is Lord of all and is generous to all who call on him. For, 'Everyone who calls on the name of the Lord shall be saved.' But how are they to call on one in whom they have not believed? And how are they to believe in one of whom they have never heard? And how are they to hear without someone to proclaim him? And how are they to proclaim him unless they are sent? As it is written, 'How beautiful are the feet of those who bring good news!'" (Romans 10:12-15). Indeed, a reminder concerning the importance of proclamation is significant to the purpose of children's meditations.

But the text and theme that perhaps most directs my thoughts in approaching children's messages is that enunciated by Jesus in declaring, "I am the bread of life. Whoever comes to me will never be hungry, and whoever believes in me will never be thirsty" (John 6:35). Indeed, it is a most compelling image and invitation. It bespeaks our great human need for nourishment. There is, of course, nothing more basic to the human body and place on earth than food and drink. Similarly, nothing is more essential to the human spirit and purpose in the world than the sustenance and refreshment of God's love. The image of feeding on God's word is, of course, foundational to the biblical narrative (Deuteronomy 8:3; Matthew 4:4). It is this sense of the need for nourishment that has led me to speak of my approach to children's meditation as a menu—a menu that endeavors to combine ingredients of biblical texts, lectionary rhythms, and seasonal themes. In so doing, I hope that this menu of meditations may prove as beneficial to others in using them as they have been to me in preparing them.

Message

A Word on Seeing Jesus

Once, during a church worship experience, my daughter turned to me and whispered, "I want to see Jesus." Her eyes wandered about the sanctuary, and she asked, "Where is Jesus?"

Her inquiry cut me to the theological quick. When I found no easy words with which to respond, she repeated her statement and her question. She was persistent; I was perplexed. How do you explain to a two-year-old, in the middle of a worship service, about seeing Jesus? She certainly was not interested in some quaint platitude or traditional rhetoric. She wanted to see Jesus. After all, that's what we had come to church to do that day, wasn't it?

"So, Dad, where's Jesus?" I looked around the sanctuary, searching for some help in responding to her earnestness. She looked for the concrete, the sensory. I found the symbolic—a cross, a table, candles, a Bible, a banner featuring the victorious lamb, a people joining in song and reading, stories and prayers.

In a sense, everything we did in the worship experience pointed to Jesus. Yet how does a two-year-old understand that? Then again, how do any of us understand it? Amidst the routines and rituals of the Christian worship endeavor, how easy it is to lose sight of what we are doing, who we are, and whom we worship. How difficult it may be to see Jesus, truly see Jesus. We may ask, with my daughter, "Where is Jesus?" And perhaps, we may even ask ourselves, "Where are the vision and vitality that make Christian worship true worship?"

That question is perhaps at the heart of the quest for church renewal in our time. Without a confession and worship centered on Christ, how can we be renewed? How can the church be drawn away from its conformity to human culture and be transformed by God's Spirit? How can we be faithful to our calling as Christians?

We recall that Jesus declared, "God is spirit, and those who worship God must worship in spirit and truth" (John 4:24). Perhaps it is this affirmation that best underscores for us the essence of our participation in worship and our quest for renewal. For in both a theological and a spiritual sense, are we not like two-year-olds seeking after the experience of Christ?

Yet the experience of Christ cannot remain at infant stages. We know that we must grow. There must be progression in our discipleship—in our worship and work. We are to become mature, not conformed to the world but transformed (*metamorphosed*) by the renewing of our minds (Romans 12:2). Such Christian maturity is rooted in Christian service, understood as both worship and mission. We are called to liturgy and labor in this life, in the name and power of Christ. It would seem, then, that the more we come to understand and embrace the essentials of such worship and work, the more we may come to experience that maturity, and thus realize a greater fulfillment of our quest to see Jesus, and to help others do so as well.

That is the premise of this book. The intention is to provide a resource to assist God's children, young and old alike, in better understanding and experiencing the gospel of Christ—the Good News of God's love. This written resource is offered as a guide, according to the church year and its narrative, for bringing concrete illustration to the spirit and symbol that so much comprise the tradition of Christian worship and inform Christian mission.

The goal is not just to explain but also to enhance. At issue is the unity and dialogue of spirit and truth in worship. The focus, then, is on providing a practical resource for telling the gospel story throughout the church year. Like worship itself, this resource constitutes a journey. Hopefully, with each season, symbol, and story, a step is taken toward enriched appreciation of the dynamic of the gospel, related through stories and images that both children and adults can understand and engage. Toward that end, each reader and practitioner is invited to embark on the journey, thereby both stepping into and contributing to the experience that we call Christian worship, toward the goal of seeing Jesus and growing in the image and mission of Christ.

A WORD ON USING THE BIBLE

The Bible is an adult book. Knowing that is a first step toward understanding and using the Bible. Such an affirmation is not to suggest that the Bible has nothing to say to children, or that one cannot communicate the message of the Bible to children. It is to say, however, that since the culture, context, and genre of the Bible are adult in content, some translation is required to make the message accessible to children. This translation begins with an understanding of the biblical message itself, but it cannot end there. In addition to devoted biblical study that seeks to understand the Bible's message through exploring its historical context, literary genre, theological content, and personal challenge, there must be a consistent attention to framing that message in terms understandable to children—and, for that matter, to youth and adults. Theology and pedagogy must walk hand in hand.

To capture the importance of this need, I speak of a "menu" of "bite-size meditations." The essence of this book is this menu. Yet any menu is very much dependent on culinary and creative preparation. There must be a method behind the menu. Thus, I need to comment a bit on that method. But first, I must comment more on the message for which there is a method. The message, of course, is that of the Scriptures. And so we return to the affirmation that the Bible is an adult book and must be approached and understood first as such.

In saying that the Bible is an adult book, we are acknowledging that it was written by and for adult members of the community of faith. It bears within it and through it a rich tapestry of God's revelation, woven together by threads and strands that have been providentially pieced together over centuries by the hearts and hands of God's faithful people. In those pieces are narratives, laws, stories, songs, symbols, propositions, poems, pictures, visions, and so many more ways of communicating God's truth and our engagement of it. We embrace the biblical affirmation "All scripture is inspired by God and is useful for teaching, for reproof, for correction, and for training in righteousness, so that everyone who belongs to God may be proficient, equipped for every good work" (2 Timothy 3:16-17).

Our study of Scripture must take stock of these many pieces of the biblical narrative as we seek to cross a chasm of history, culture, language, and genre. This is no easy undertaking for adults; it is far more challenging for children. We may take heart from the Bible's own admission that the writings of Scripture contain some things that are "hard to understand" (2 Peter 3:16), and we might also be cautioned that our understanding of Scripture cannot be just a matter of individualistic interpretation (2 Peter 1:20).

While it is certainly beyond the scope of this book to unfold the particulars and parameters of an approach to biblical study and interpretation, it must be said that a devotion to such study, interpretation, and application of Scripture is assumed. Only on the basis of such is sharing the biblical message with children a viable and vital enterprise. One does not have to be a biblical scholar, but one does have to be a biblical student. The opportunity for sharing the biblical message is always rooted in an ongoing study of that message. Having identified that assumption, I may now say a word about the manner of using the Bible with children.

"One does not have to be a biblical scholar,
but one does have to be a biblical student."

One of the temptations in using the Bible with children is to make the Bible into a collection of morality tales, as if the biblical canon is a compendium of cute and quaint stories. This approach entails some variation of telling a so-called Bible story and concluding with a nearly stereotypical "and the moral of the story is" ending. Yet this approach often distorts, even cheapens, the biblical message. The biblical message is complex and usually much deeper than the superficial storyline that we are tempted to abstract from its overall narrative. Sharing a biblical message with anyone, but especially children, entails both a faithful summation of the biblical meaning and a thoughtful communication of that meaning. Such messages, then, ought not to be pedestrian, moralistic, or oversimplified. Instead, they should be characterized as clear and concise and creative, reflective and recited and recycled. Let me comment briefly on what I mean by these.

BE CLEAR, CONCISE, AND CREATIVE

First, sharing a biblical message starts with being clear. That, of course, assumes that the message is clear for the messenger. If our own understanding is fuzzy, so likely will our sharing of that message be. This is not to suggest that we need to be masters of the biblical message in all its diversity and complexity. It does suggest, however, that we need to be focused on what we wish to communicate.

Second, sharing a bite-size meditation implies that the message needs to be concise. No message can share all that the Bible has to say, even on one subject. If one pitfall is oversimplifying the biblical message, another is trying to pack an overview of the whole Bible into every brief message. Bite-size means manageable in both scope and subject. We must limit how much we say and be clear on what we say.

Being clear and concise, then, entails a precision and brevity of focus. We cannot say everything, but we can say something. That something is significant. We must ever remember that. Inasmuch as that something is pinpointed by us in preparing our presentation, it can more readily be perceived and received by those with whom the message is shared. That, indeed, is the point of being clear and concise.

Finally, note that it is important to identify our audience and to be straightforward and creative in sharing our message with that audience. Being straightforward carries the sense of "to the point," but also "down to earth" and accessible. The intent is to share a message by proceeding in a straight course. The message is to be candid and connected to the audience. To be connected is to be clear about the audience we are addressing and creative in helping the message be received with understanding. To be candid is to be focused and creative in framing the message in terms of common, everyday experience. This is where the use of illustration and analogy is critical for children's messages. I will say more about this in the next section on undertaking children's messages. For now, let it suffice for me to make a comment on the importance of being connected to our audience.

We must consider the age, experience, and background of our audience. For instance, for the meditations included in this collection, I have assumed a range of language experience of ages four to twelve. At the same time, I have sought to advance a message relevant to youth and adults, while still being understandable by the children's age group. This may be a broader range of audience than is appropriate for some children's meditations, but it acknowledges the fact that, generally speaking, everyone is listening. So, let's speak to all. Some people may understand and engage certain parts of the message more than other parts. Children, youth, and adults may receive slightly different messages from the one message. This is really no different than what typically occurs with a Sunday sermon; people engage the message from their vantage point of experience and need. Recognizing this reality allows us to present the message in as clear, concise, and creative a fashion as possible, with the full knowledge, even expectation, that God's Spirit works to impart that message to responsive hearts based on people's openness, experiences, and needs.

The Bible is filled with complexities. Crossing the chasms of history, culture, and language is not done simply. Yet it must be done, and we must be creative in doing so. This means that we must be careful not to become bogged down in the minutia of textual and critical questions and challenges. We may do well to wrestle with such inquiries as part of our own study and interpretation of Scripture. The message we share, however, needs to be forthright and straightforward in communicating a clear theme. While we do not want to over-simplify the message, and thereby deprive it of its authenticity and vitality, we also do not want to become overly preoccupied with its less primary particulars. Such preoccupation, if allowed, may well cause us not to be able to see the forest for the trees. Our purpose is best served by focusing on those central components of the message that are clear in content and that need to be made clear in communication. I will say a bit more, subsequently, on the subject of being creative. But first, let me underscore one more key point in our use of Scripture.

REFLECT AND RECITE AND RECYCLE

Throughout the seasons of the church year, and the children's messages therein, we seek to be faithful to the biblical narrative with which we work. This entails wrestling with and sharing the meaning of individual Scripture passages. This is the reflection part of our preparation and presentation. We seek to reflect upon the Scripture's meaning during our preparation, and then to reflect that message in our presentation to the children and congregation. Also included is our effort to express the manifold witness of Scripture from week to week and season to season. This is the recital aspect to our communication. Each message is part of an ongoing reiteration of the drama of God's love revealed in Scripture and unfolding in our lives. The seasons of the church year are an attempt to recycle the word of salvation, making it fresh with each Scripture lesson. No single Scripture passage or theme encapsulates the entire biblical message, and yet each Scripture is part and parcel of its comprehensive drama. Both the specifics of a single text and the scope of the entire canon must be in our view. Our messages, then, are best collected and communicated according to some ongoing, unfolding, systematic, and wide-ranging wrestling with the Bible.

Each message is part of an ongoing reiteration of the drama of God's love revealed in Scripture and unfolding in our lives.

The traditional lectionary rotation of Scripture lessons is a prime example of such an approach. Its use combines both the reflection and recital we seek to engage. The lectionary, of course, includes a three-year order of Scripture lessons (designated as Years A, B, C). Ordered according to the seasons and themes of the church year, Scripture readings include four passages of Scripture each week, typically taken from the First Testament (Hebrew Scriptures), the Psalms, the New Testament Epistles, and the Gospels. Central to such an approach to Scripture reading is an affirmation of both the seasonally relevant themes and broad scope of the biblical narrative.

The lectionary is the organizing principle according to which I have compiled the menu of messages in this book. In using the lectionary I am not suggesting that it is the only means of ordering meditations, but I am commending it as a very useful and ecumenical means of doing so. The menu of meditations in this book has been indexed by lectionary readings, along with Scripture references, seasons of the church year, and general themes and topics, in hopes of making the lessons as accessible and useful as possible.

At issue is our use of Scripture and understanding of its message. The use of Scripture in a broad-ranged systematic manner serves to force our imagination in many directions, and not just toward those familiar paths, those same steps, those comfortable places we find in a limited number of Scripture texts and themes. Often, we simply indulge that which makes us comfortable. This is a natural temptation. Yet in indulging only our own choice of texts, the content we present may be unchallenging, for it reinforces our complacency rather than awakens our conscience. At the heart of recital is repetition, and at the heart of pedagogy is reiteration of theme. A seasonal and thematic approach to Scripture helps us tackle and teach the biblical lessons in an ongoing and comprehensive manner. By precluding us from a narrow encounter with Scripture, the lectionary (or some other systematic approach to Scripture) prompts us to engage the full range of biblical themes, topics, concerns, and challenges. Herein, we are able to study and share the central motifs of Scripture in a comprehensive and continuous manner.

"Yet in indulging only our own choice of texts, the content we present may be unchallenging, for it reinforces our complacency rather than awakens our conscience."

These central motifs fill the Scriptures and seasons of the church year, and hence our children's messages. The biblical narrative is a long and winding road that recites and recycles the message of God's love. We can do no better in our children's messages than to recite and recycle that message. Scripture and tradition are filled with recital. Recital is important to reflection and response. We need not shy away from repeating themes at different times and through different Scriptures. Themes of God's light and love, our growth and calling, the promises of love and forgiveness, the challenges of peace and justice—all these are the fabric of the biblical drama. They ought naturally to be woven again and again into our stories and meditations, even as they fill the pages and epochs of Scripture. The repetition of themes, illustrations, symbols, and subjects is an important reinforcement of the overriding message of Scripture: God loves us and invites us to the journey of love with God and neighbor.

"The biblical narrative is a long and winding road that recites and recycles the message of God's love."

Method

A Word on Undertaking Children's Messages

Having affirmed the biblical message and discussed some of the concerns and challenges related to using Scripture, let me now highlight a few points that are significant to our ability to communicate the message of the Scripture to the children with whom we minister. I sometimes refer to this as the "Pray, Prepare, Share" approach to children's messages. It bespeaks a methodology for the message we seek to communicate. The following comments, then, are offered as a brief overview of some of the essential points to bear in mind when presenting children's meditations.

Pray, Prepare, Share

Pray. The first aspect of preparation is prayer. Not a quick, last-moment prayer just before the children's time on Sunday morning, but rather, an ongoing attitude and approach of prayer that brings you into a meditative mood toward God and the Scripture and theme with which you are wrestling. Assume that God will be there for the message. Affirm God's presence and commit your preparation to God's care. As the psalmist exhorts, "Commit your way to Yahweh; trust in God, and God will act" (Psalm 37:5). Anticipate good things from yourself and God, as well as from the children gathered together for a few moments. In this respect, prayer is not simply a brief action, but an ongoing attitude of approach. You may also choose to include a brief vocal prayer at the end of the message as a way to thank God for being part of the sharing.

Plan ahead. Do not wait until the night before; prepare at least a week in advance. That way, you can think about the message and picture it in your mind throughout the week. In this respect, there is a clear advantage in the lectionary, as the biblical passages are set before you a year in advance. Other approaches to organizing Scriptures and themes, however, may be utilized. Intentional links to seasonal themes, sermons, hymns, songs, prayers, and other aspects of the worship may be made from week to week. This, of course, requires planning ahead.

In planning, you become prepared. Envision what you will say and how you will say it. For some people, it may be helpful to write out the message. This is especially effective in making sure you use child-friendly language and keep your message to a reasonable length. Toward that end, I have offered a narrative of each lesson for each week's meditation collected in this book. Preparation is a combination of intellectual, spiritual, emotional, and social readiness. By planning ahead, you will be prepared to be effective, and you will enjoy yourself and your time with the children a great deal more.

"In planning, you become prepared."

Share out of your own experience and understanding. You don't have to be an expert. You just need a heart. Ongoing biblical study is an important part of your preparation, yes. But a children's message is not a scholarly lecture. It is a personal sharing. Share what you know. Share from your heart. Be natural and not stilted. If you are relaxed and are having a good time, the children will do likewise.

Share a relationship, not just words. The biblical message is more than words; it is relationship. At the heart of sharing the gospel is a relationship. Your ongoing and unfolding relationship with the children and congregation is not peripheral. It is a vital part of the incarnational communication of God's word of love. Nurture that relationship, even as you prepare for the message itself. Sometimes in the course of your communication with the children, the words and message may seem to get a bit lost. But if the relationship is further nurtured, you have gained just the same, and so have the children. For in this you incarnate the message.

The key communication is a caring embrace of the children themselves. We recall the words of Jesus about welcoming children: "Let the little children come to me, and do not stop them; for it is to such as these that the kingdom of God belongs. Truly I tell you, whoever does not receive the kingdom of God as a little child will never enter it" (Luke 18:16-17). By welcoming children, we bless them. By sharing with them, we express caring for them. So, feel free to be yourself, that you may reach out and welcome the children and thereby communicate care for them. As a result, the children sense that they are acknowledged as an indispensable part of the community of faith. They are special. Their place and participation in the worship and mission of the church is affirmed as vital.

"The key communication is a caring embrace of the children themselves."

As your relationship with them is nurtured, their sense of belonging to the family of God is nurtured. Herein, beyond the specific words of a message, a reality of relationship is fostered. The children are affirmed as we communicate caring. In addition to the specifics of the individual message each week, our consistent message is that the children are important to God and special to us in worship. They belong to God and to God's family. We need them, and so we let them know. Furthermore, each week memories may hereby be created, not primarily out of the words of a particular lesson, but out of the relationship of love being shared.

Share with enthusiasm. If you want the children to be interested, you have to be interesting. First and foremost that means you need to be enthusiastic about the sharing time. If you come across as indifferent, then don't be surprised if the children are indifferent too. You don't have to entertain the children, but you need to engage them. Enthusiasm engages. It's never just routine. It's shaped by a bit of excitement and surprise. So, get excited about the message, the children, the occasion, or some other aspect. Sometimes it's difficult for adults to step out of what often is a stuffy, adult role. This time with the children should certainly give us permission to do so. Make the time with the children enlivened. I sense that as this brief time is enlivened, it serves to help enliven the whole worship experience for the congregation. At the least, the time with the children should remind us all that central to our worship gathering is a celebration of the friendship, fun, and fellowship we can share as God's family. What better occasion for taking "seriously" the Apostle Paul's exhortation "My brothers and sisters, rejoice in the Lord. . . . Rejoice in the Lord always; again I will say, Rejoice" (Philippians 3:1; 4:4).

Be Inclusive and Inviting

Affirm the children as important to the worship experience. The children's message should have a significant place in the worship, preferably as part of the lesson time, in conjunction with the Scripture readings and sermon. Invite the children to come forward or to listen from their seats. Not all children will come forward, but they may well still listen from their seats. Be sure to gesture and offer eye contact with both those gathered with you and those throughout the congregation. By your attention to them, wherever they are seated, you let them know that they are important, and that you are glad they are present and participating in worship. The point is to draw a gathering circle, as it were, that includes and not excludes. In this respect, I suggest that it's good to avoid having the children's message be a prelude to sending the children out of worship. If your worship service doesn't include children for the whole time, then try alternative ways to dismiss children, such as during a hymn. You don't want to communicate to children that the message is just a step toward separating them from the larger worship experience. They may well then be focused on what's coming up next rather than the message at hand.

"The point is to draw a gathering circle ..."

Use inclusive language. Inclusive language helps both boys and girls feel included. Tell stories, use objects, cite examples, and so forth that will appeal to both genders, as well as to a variety of ages. Sometimes this means that you have to expand the storyline a bit. Broaden it so everyone can fit into it. This way, everyone will feel that they belong and that they have a place in the sharing.

Speak inclusively of God as "God." Avoid referring to God as "He" or "It." Using personal pronouns for God can suggest to children that God has gender. Be careful not to overuse titles like "Creator" or "Savior," which may not be fully understandable to children. If you want to use these titles, you may need to help illustrate what they mean. For example, if I don't know what a carpenter is, I may not understand what you are saying if you talk about a carpenter. But if you talk about a person who builds things with wood, then I can follow the story. Speaking of God in inclusive, concrete, and symbolic ways can help nurture a growing understanding of God's mysterious and loving nature.

While we wish to affirm and nurture personal relationship with God, we must always be cognizant of the reality of God's mystery. We should be comfortable with speaking of God often in illustrative terms, advancing that "God is like ..." For this indeed is a pattern we find time and again in the Scriptures, wherein God is described in anthropomorphic terms. The parables of Jesus, for instance, picture God in many ways: a conscientious and caring shepherd, a diligent woman, a loving father (Luke 15). The creation account describes God as hovering like a hen in a nest at the birth of the world (Genesis 1:2). We are reminded that God is Spirit (John 4:24). There is mystery in God's person and presence. While we wish to underscore God's loving presence, we ought not banish God's mystery through oversimplification. In this respect, the importance of Jesus in revealing God personally, as well as prophetically, is crucial for our understanding and sharing. We recall the promise of Jesus: "For where two or three are gathered in my name, I am there among them" (Matthew 18:20).

"There is mystery in God's person and presence."

Part of a good invitation is a good spot to gather. Usually this will be at the front of the worship setting. It should be a place from which you can be heard and the children can be seen. The gathering place should be easy to get to and comfortable for everyone. The value of a gathering place is that it helps create a sense of ownership and belonging by the children. The gathering, then, bespeaks a place that is special, even sacred. A consistent time for the gathering may also be helpful, though this very much depends on the overall style of the worship. A varied gathering time may be more suitable for some worship approaches.

FOLLOW THE LECTIONARY OR OTHER RHYTHM OF SCRIPTURE READINGS

Follow a rhythm of Scripture-based lessons for your messages. A measure of continuity from week to week is helpful in building on lessons with the children. As we have noted, the lectionary works well for this. One advantage of the lectionary is that the Scripture readings are set out in advance (according to a three-year cycle of readings). Another advantage of the lectionary is that it offers four choices of Scripture each week. Choose one, and base your children's message on a key part of that Scripture lesson.

These advantages help both you and the congregation prepare. As advance notice of Scripture lessons is made (through the worship bulletin or church newsletter), members of the congregation have the option of becoming better prepared for the worship experience through their own reflection on the texts. Such texts, of course, can be announced in advance (a week, a month, or a season at a time), whether or not they are part of the lectionary rotation. In other words, this approach is flexible with whatever way Scripture texts and sermon themes are selected for weekly worship. Your planning ahead, coupled with the congregation's looking ahead, gives everyone something to anticipate. This then reinforces our sense that important biblical themes require ongoing attention and are unfolded throughout the year. Our intent is to live God's word. We know we cannot learn it all in one session. We need to think, ponder, feel, fashion, pray, practice, live, breathe, and act on God's word in our midst. Looking at and living with Scripture texts for more than a day at a time greatly enhances this process of learning.

"Our intent is to live God's word."

In the Menu section that follows in this book, you will find that each sermon is prefaced by suggested Scripture texts and the relevant lectionary days. Where more than one of these is listed, the texts and Scriptures are placed in the same order. In other words, if the suggestions are listed as follows:

Scripture: John 3:7-8; John 4:24
Lectionary Day: Second Sunday in Lent, Year A; Third
                  Sunday in Lent, Year A

then the first Scripture text is linked to the first lectionary day. Where more than one Scripture is listed for a single lectionary day, those texts will be designated as follows (highlighted in bold typeface below):

Scripture: Matthew 21:1-11; **Mark 11:1-11** or **John 12:12-19;** Luke 19:28-40

Lectionary Day: Palm/Passion Sunday, Year A; **Palm/Passion Sunday, Year B;** Palm/Passion Sunday Year C

Where a Scripture is included in the lectionary readings for more than one day in the church year, that fact is represented by including the secondary day in italicized parentheses following the primary day, as shown below in bold typeface:

Scripture: Psalm 96; **Psalm 98;** Psalm 149

Lectionary Day: Christmas Day, Years A, B, C; **Christmas Day, Year A;** *(also Sixth Sunday of the Resurrection, Year B);* All Saints' Day, Year C

Indexes of liturgical days, Scriptures, and message themes may be found at the end of this book to further facilitate your selection or creation of messages relevant to the church year.

Even if you are not following the lectionary readings of Scripture, keep your messages pertinent to the liturgical season. Choose Scriptures that are in keeping with the themes of Advent, Epiphany, Lent, and so forth. Messages tied to the worship season help reinforce both the season and your message for the children, as a variety of themes are woven together into a more complete picture. Scripture and season are partners in sharing God's voice with us. The voice of Scripture is heard in biblical and liturgical rhythms.

The Bible confronts us with God and often brings us into conflict with our wider human culture. Attuning ourselves to biblical and liturgical rhythms, rather than being conformed to cultural norms and themes, serves to heighten our focus on God. We seek to encounter God's voice in the regular rhythm of biblical lessons and seasonal themes. In this respect, integration is important to the worship experience and reinforces the meaning of the meditation. The season, Scriptures, lessons, songs, and decorations all contribute to the overall effect of the message and our engagement of it in the worship context. I will comment a bit more on the seasonal themes of the church year in the final part of this section on method.

"The Bible confronts us with God and often brings us into conflict with our wider human culture."

SPEAK SO CHILDREN CAN UNDERSTAND

Be brief. If your message is more than four or five minutes long, you may lose some of your listeners. Children have short attention spans. The children's message should be enthusiastic in tone, colorful in language, and to the point. Don't belabor your message. Say it and be done. Some messages demand more explanation than others, but the overall point should be clear enough to be grasped and engaged by the children without excessive explanation. It is often effective to present meditations as a kind of storytelling, where one point flows into another. I often think of the process as painting a picture, with each stroke adding more color and detail.

Typically, use words and sentence structure that a five-year-old can understand. Yes, the adults want to hear the message, but don't speak directly to them. Speak to the children in their own language. You don't have to talk down to children, but you should use words within their range of vocabulary. If you speak beyond their ability to comprehend, you will forfeit the opportunity for growth. Language is critical to learning. It is not words but growth that we advance. It is not that we simply share information; we seek transformation.

Learning proceeds from the known to the new. We move from what we know to what is new. We build on the known in embracing the new. The key aspect in the communication is discernment. As communicators, we must discern where the children and congregation are in the journey, help them identify what they know, and then make connections to their next step—moving to the new. This is pursued through dialogue, sharing, repetition, and reinforcement. As such, learning is a tapestry that requires many threads being contributed and woven together.

"Learning proceeds from the known to the new."

Avoid theological clichés and pious platitudes. Children don't understand such language, and it often gets in the way of the message. Adults will also tune out, since they feel that they have heard it all before. If a five- or a six-year-old cannot tell you what a word means, it is probably best not to use it, unless you help define it in the course of the message. Indeed, there are occasions that require introducing new terminology, such as biblical vocabulary or theological concepts. Following the guideline of moving from the known to the new helps a great deal in framing how to cover new territory.

Ask questions. Get the children thinking. You don't have to give them an inordinate amount of time to answer. Rhetorical questions are helpful in that they prompt attentiveness and yet keep the meditation focused. The lesson is not a free-for-all discussion. Sometimes just a quick question that you almost answer yourself is better than an open-ended inquiry. Just a quick nod from the children is sufficient. Likewise, your brief gesture toward them lets them know that you care about their response, while at the same time being clear that you are not inviting conversation that may be tangential to the focus. Acknowledging the children's attentiveness through eye contact, nods, and gestures of affirmation and agreement are sufficient to keep the lesson unfolding. It is best not to leave long silences. Avoid giving that budding three-year-old preacher too much time to wax eloquently. Try to keep the meditation moving. Do not get bogged down in details, but emphasize the overall theme. If something does not flow or go over quite as you expected, then rephrase, re-direct, and keep proceeding. Remember, the key is the overall message, not all the details.

Tell stories. Share in conversation. Children can follow messages that have a beginning and ending. Your message should be tied together like a ribbon wrapping a package. Try not to leave loose ends. If something doesn't contribute to the flow of the story, avoid using it. Move the message along. Presenting it like a story helps a great deal. Since much of the biblical material is in narrative form, often you are called not to invent a story but to translate one that is given in Scripture.

Use Picture Language and Illustration

Paint pictures with your words. Use colorful words. Describe what you are saying. Talk is not enough. We must envision the message and then paint a picture for the children. Give them images and opportunities to see what you are saying. By both seeing and hearing, they will better be able to remember what you said. The image will stay with them long after the word has been lost. The adage about a picture being worth a thousand words is very true for children.

Make use of metaphor as a window of illustration. Essentially this means making use of comparisons and illustrations. As a learner, what I know helps me see what I can learn. As educators, we seek to help students move from the known to the new. This can often best be done through the use of metaphor, analogies, illustrations, and examples. In explaining something new, we start with something known. This empowers our listeners to begin the journey with confidence. Metaphor prepares for movement. We open the pathway for insight and growth by providing metaphorical pictures that help the children (as well as the adults) understand the new learning in terms of previously known learning. Metaphor facilitates this movement because it points simultaneously to what people know and what they are about to learn. That is, they can see in two directions and are empowered to use what they know to tackle what is new. Providing people with illustrations not only gives them confidence for the learning journey, but also helps them understand the connection to their life. Herein, the content and context are wedded. This power of metaphor rests with the teacher's ability to paint pictures and provide illustrations for the listeners.

"Metaphor prepares for movement."

Make use of object lessons. An object lesson is a message built around an object you have brought to share. As children look at the object, you describe it and use it as a springboard to talk about the message you wish to share. The Bible, in parables and prophetic visions, is filled with descriptions drawn from the world of nature and human experience. There are many ready-made objects that can augment a lesson. Sometimes the object may serve as a good introduction to the topic and story being presented. Other times, however, the illustration may be integrated into the middle of the meditation. There is always a cautionary note that must be attached to so-called object lessons. In using objects, we must be careful not to overemphasize the object and thereby slight the lesson itself. It is perilously easy to focus more on the object and miss the point of the meditation. Objects are not the lesson; they only help illustrate it.

Make use of analogies. An analogy is when you compare something new to something already known. An analogy can make use of an object, but it also can simply refer to something that children already know about (even though you don't have an object illustrating it right there). When you want to communicate something new for children to think about and maybe act upon, you can relate it to something they already know about. In this way, their understanding builds on what is familiar and proceeds to what is new and inviting.

Using analogy requires imagination and creativity. It means that we must be prepared and able to move outside the boundaries of a subject at any moment in order to cite or create an analogy, illustration, or example that will help clarify the learning focus. All in all, analogies and illustrations provide access to insight and learning. They are like on-ramps; but they also include revisiting, reminding, and renewing, and thus are like pit stops and rest areas. The power and process of using analogy in our lessons continually seeks to paint pictures that increasingly unfold clearer views and closer understandings of God and God's love.

EMBRACE SYMBOLS FROM AND FOR THE WORSHIP SETTING

Most Christian worship settings have a variety of symbols and symbolic furnishings. These make ready reference points and illustrations for our weekly meditations. Of course, as noted above, we should use objects and symbols to enhance the message, not substitute for it. Yet the symbols that fill our worship setting abound with deep meanings to be explored. They are like texts just waiting for commentary. Therefore, make use of symbols. Although most worship settings are filled with symbols, children understand very few of them, and even many of the adults have lost the meaning of some of them. Explain things from time to time. This helps both children and adults understand the symbols of the worship setting. How come the pulpit and Communion table are so prominent? What's that "IHS" on the tablecloth? Why do we have a cross, a banner, candles, and so forth here and there? What about the worship colors that change from season to season?

"Symbols ... are like texts just waiting for commentary."

In referencing symbols, be mindful of the season of the year. The liturgical year suggests appropriate themes. In making use of them, you reinforce the other aspects of worship (music, decoration, etc.) in highlighting the point you are trying to emphasize. Making use of liturgical symbols is a great way further to integrate the weekly meditation with weekly worship.

Integration of illustration and meditation within the overall life of the congregation is an added benefit of utilizing symbols. When citing or commenting on a specific symbol, be intentional about making connections with the Sunday school, fellowship, and mission life of the congregation as well. Such connections provide links to the larger life of the church family. In addition, they may open the door for creating an extended conversation and dialogue on the lesson. In this respect, I think there is value in creating one's own symbols from time to time in presenting the children's message. Sometime this may simply mean introducing something associated with your illustration and placing it temporarily but prominently in the worship setting. Other times it entails creating something to share—a banner, a poster, a sign, and so forth. These give the children something additional to see, remember, even keep, and recall when subsequent lessons unfold. These symbolic items can then perhaps be links to further follow-up and relationship with the children outside the worship environment. In this sense, symbols constitute seeds for further sowing and growing.

REMEMBER THAT ADULTS ARE LISTENING TOO

Speak to everyone. Speak loudly and clearly enough for adults to hear as well. Even though your message is to the children, and should be on their terms, it is also inevitably being shared with everyone. So, you should try to acknowledge the youth and adults by speaking to them a bit also. Having the special time with the children is not meant to segregate the children or to exclude the youth and adults. Our intent is to be inclusive. We want to help the children feel special, but we also need to acknowledge the adults. I have commented on how the Bible is an adult book; our goal is to make it more accessible to children. A by-product of that effort is helping the adults as well. In this way, a sense of learning and community is nurtured among all.

Worship, of course, is for everyone, and it is inextricably connected to the experiences of learning and community. The children's moment is an opportunity to nurture the bonds between children and adults and help them be better connected. The point is to nurture a sense of belonging. An experience of fun, fellowship, faith, and family is central to our purpose in the children's meditation. Herein, we seek and share the vision of God's family wherein "the whole group of those who believed were of one heart and soul" (Acts 4:32).

"An experience of fun, fellowship, faith, and family is central to our purpose in the children's meditation."

Interject humor. Humor and good feelings help your message. Both adults and children can respond and feel included. Humor also helps people relax and be less anxious. You want the experience to be relaxed and enjoyable for the whole congregation. I have always felt that humor is chief among the aids to the spirit of teaching. Wit and wisdom must be allies. There is a saying that asserts, "Things work out best for those who make the best out of the way things work out." This is certainly true for children's meditations. In leading the children and congregation we must feature and foster a sense of humor that allows the learning process to be fun, unafraid of failure, ready for adjustments, and flexible enough to bend and not break among the stresses and challenges of communication.

Be flexible. If something doesn't go exactly as you planned, take it in stride. If the children don't respond much, or perhaps too much, or not exactly as you had anticipated, do not worry about it. A little humor, shrugging of shoulders, or other gestures that indicate you are comfortable with the twists and turns will help everyone be comfortable. Turning mistakes and the unpredictable moments into fun opportunities goes a long way in nurturing a sense of community among everyone—children and adults alike. And after all, that's half of what we are trying to accomplish in the first place!

A WORD ON THE SEASONS OF THE CHRISTIAN YEAR

As we have underscored the value of the seasonal rhythms of Scripture readings and worship themes in the Christian year, it is appropriate to comment briefly on the subject as a whole. The Christian church year provides a unique perspective for viewing and following the flow of a year. It is not simply liturgical in nature; it is also very much theological, educational, and ethical. In a sense, it is an annual drama of salvation history and the time of the church. Salvation history bespeaks the intent and action of God's love as unfolded in human history and in human hearts. The time of the church is that epoch, and its calling, between the resurrection and return of Christ. Thus, the Christian year is markedly Christ-centered. With the advent of God in Christ, a new day dawns, and we seek to live in the light of that new day. In annual recital, we learn of God's love in Christ and learn to follow Christ in love and life.

The Christian year offers a distinctive way to measure and order time. It is different from that represented in the calendar year. Likewise, its days and themes are different from those included in the national culture. Holy days are distinct from holidays. It may be a temptation to mix in days that are national and cultural in nature with those of the Christian year; to yield to that temptation frequently results in a distraction that minimizes our attentiveness to the distinctly Christian themes of the year. In following the flow of the Christian year and its sacred seasons, the intent is to nurture our faith through the recital of the events and experiences of salvation that Scripture and our church life afford us. Inasmuch as the children's meditation participates in this recital, it underscores for children the importance of God's presence and priorities, which often stand in contrast to those of the wider culture and its values.

"Holy days are distinct from holidays."

The Christian year begins on the first Sunday of Advent, which is calculated as four Sundays before Christmas Day. The traditional liturgical color for Advent is purple, with blue as a more recent alternative. The color is used in symbol of royalty, meditation, penitence, and preparedness, in keeping with the predominant themes of the Advent season. In both biblical text and music, Advent is an anticipatory time that speaks of promise, preparation, hope, and fulfillment. It weaves together a look back to Christ's nativity and a look forward to Christ's return. It underscores our need and hope for God's intervention in human history, and stresses our being ready to embrace and participate in the "new thing" that God may yet accomplish.

Christmas is the festival of the incarnation, God's promised presence fulfilled in the human existence of Jesus. As Advent is a time of expectation, Christmas is a time of celebration. Its celebration is prepared for in Advent, which precedes it, and then is reflected in Epiphany, which follows it. Christmas follows the four Sundays in Advent, and is observed for twelve days, between December 25 and January 6, Epiphany. The liturgical color, beginning on Christmas Eve, is white, with gold as an alternative. The color symbolizes the purity, victory, and celebration of Christmas. The celebration of God's presence and promise is paramount. Highlighting the words of Isaiah, we affirm that "God is with us." It is a time to exult in God's glory and love as revealed in Jesus.

Furthermore, it is a time to have renewed within us the glory of love that we may share with one another.

The season of Epiphany begins January 6 and continues until Ash Wednesday. Typically, the color for the day of Epiphany and the Sunday that follows is white, depending on the specific liturgical tradition being followed. The season continues much of the same celebration themes of Christmas. A special focus on God's light as manifested in Christ and through Christ to the world is characteristic of the season. Epiphany is variously observed in church traditions in remembrance of the visit of the magi and in recital of the baptism of Jesus. In either case, the theme centers on the manifestation of Christ to the nations. In the Sundays after Epiphany Sunday the liturgical color usually is green, though some traditions continue with white. It is a season for celebrating and exploring the impact of God's light in our lives.

The season of Lent commences with Ash Wednesday. The day is calculated forty days prior to Palm Sunday, in commemoration of the forty days of Jesus' temptation. The Sundays in this period are called Lent (from the Old English word for "lengthen"). The color for the Sundays in Lent is violet, in symbolism of the meditation and penitence associated with the Lenten season. This season invites us to a special engagement of God through confession, prayer, fasting, and study. While the season is clearly more somber than others, it anticipates the saving activity of God in the death and resurrection of Christ. Thus, the season underscores the ministry and teachings of Jesus and our personal response through discipleship. In this, Lent is the gateway to Holy Week.

Holy Week is the week from Palm/Passion Sunday to Holy Saturday. It concludes Lent while it ushers us to Resurrection Sunday. Included in Holy Week are Maundy Thursday, Good Friday, and Holy Saturday. The color for Palm Sunday remains purple, though red is sometimes used. Likewise, for Maundy Thursday the color is purple, with red as an alternative. The color for Good Friday often is brown or black, with red or no color at all as alternatives. This week is a unique time of reflection upon the life, suffering, death, and sacrifice of Christ. It beckons us to ponder how the passion of Christ fulfills the purpose of God, and it beseeches us to consider how our own commitment to the service of love and justice may emanate from this "wondrous love," as the traditional hymn affirms.

The Day of Resurrection, commonly called Easter Sunday, begins a seven-week season in celebration of Christ's resurrection. It is the highpoint of the Christian worship year. In the Western church this day is calculated as the first Sunday after the first full moon following the vernal equinox. The colors for the season of Resurrection are white and gold. Ascension Day is forty days after Resurrection Sunday. Hence, it is always on a Thursday in the week following the sixth Sunday of Resurrection. Its colors also are white and gold, in keeping with the themes of divinity and celebration that characterize the season of Resurrection. The joy of God's victory and the universality of God's love are predominant themes. The Good News of new life is clearly an appropriate focus for worship, preaching, and children's meditations.

Pentecost Sunday is ten days later, always the eighth Sunday after Resurrection Sunday. Its color is red, in symbolism of the fire and tongues associated with the Spirit's descent upon the early church. This time features a celebration and consideration of God's Spirit and God's family, the church. Trinity Sunday follows the week after Pentecost. Its theme is the Triune God, and usually its color is white. Pentecost and Trinity Sundays provide a focus that assists us in understanding the varied work of God and in embracing the vocation of God's people. Highlighting the community of faith, then, is an appropriate way to underscore God's continuing work of salvation in people's lives.

The Sundays following Pentecost and Trinity Sunday are considered the season of "ordinary time" in the church year. There are no festival periods in this long season of the church year. The basic color of green, in variation of earth-tones, is associated with the season as a symbol of growth. Typical themes include, for example, discipleship, church, mission, and stewardship. This lengthy time of the Christian year invites exploration of many themes associated with the Christian life and mission. A number of Sundays within this period may have an alternate color in keeping with a specific remembrance or observance. For instance, Reformation Sunday, the last Sunday in October, usually employs red in symbol of the zeal of the Spirit. Likewise, All Saints' Sunday, the first Sunday of November, uses red in symbol of the saints and martyrs, though some traditions employ white in symbol of purity and holiness.

The last Sunday of the worship year is that before the first Sunday in Advent. This Sunday is the Reign of Christ (or Christ the King/Sovereign) Sunday. Its focus is the ministry, triumph, and sovereignty of Christ. It highlights our anticipation of God's purpose of right relationship coming to fruition as the goal of history. The focus is the reign of God in Christ. In this manner, this Sunday summarizes in one day what the entire church year has endeavored to recite. The liturgical color for this Sunday often is white; however, many times this Sunday is also the Sunday immediately prior to the American Thanksgiving, and so some traditions prefer to employ the color red, which frequently is associated with harvest and other dedication occasions.

In sum, the Christian year is a rhythm of liturgy and life focusing on the saving events of Christ. There are essentially six basic liturgical seasons, each with a color to signify it. Advent utilizes purple/blue in symbol of Christ's royalty and our preparation. Christmas is characterized by white/gold as celebration colors, and Epiphany uses white/green. The season of Lent utilizes violet in symbol of penitence. The Resurrection season employs white/gold in symbol of divinity and celebration. Pentecost and other days throughout the year associated with dedication, zeal, and martyrdom usually employ red. The ordinary time following Pentecost makes use of green and earth-tones in symbol of life and growth.

"The Christian year is a rhythm of liturgy and life focusing on the saving events of Christ."

The menu of meditations contained in this book represents an assortment of Sunday lessons keyed to the seasons and themes of the church year. This in no way means that their use is limited to those seasons, for they are indexed by topic and Scripture text as well. Nevertheless, the intent is to demonstrate an appropriate consistency with the Christian seasons and holy days through the preparation and presentation of each children's meditation.

MENU

ADVENT AND CHRISTMAS

STIRRING UP LOVE

Scripture: 1 Thessalonians 3:9-13
Lectionary Day: First Sunday of Advent, Year C
Topic: God's Love; Loving Others
Illustration: Bellows (as used for a home fireplace or
                  woodstove)

Overview:

Emphasis on the season of Advent as a time of preparation for celebrating Christmas is a traditional theme of Advent. The most important part of preparation, of course, is our hearts. God wants to fill us with love and stir us up with love, so that we can celebrate the birth of Jesus and share God's love with others. This lesson seeks to underscore that theme by illustrating it through reference to using bellows, which for some children, and many adults, is associated with wood-stoves in operation for winter cold.

Explain how bellows work to stir up a fire in a woodstove. Then make comparison to how God wants to stir love up in us as we prepare to celebrate Christmas. As an ending, it may be helpful to use the song "Pass It On." The first verse is appropriate, as it asserts that a warming fire begins with just a spark. This verse, with appropriate permission from the copyright holder, might even be printed in the worship bulletin for easy reference. It would also be helpful if using this song to be sure to have a few adults, maybe the choir, prompted to join in with you immediately in singing the song. This will both assist the children and encourage the congregation as a whole to join together.

As with most children's sermons, it is important not to leave open-ended questions hanging for children to grab and move in a different direction than the lesson intends. That is, the use of rhetorical questions and questions that can be responded to by the children in nods, rather than extended comment, is helpful in keeping the lesson brief, to the point, and moving toward the intended goal. This part of the dialogue, however, is always a delicate point. While, on the one hand, we want to invite the children's active participation, we do not want, on the other hand, to let go of the reins of direction for the lesson. This means that verbal responses from children should be elicited and affirmed as brief. Their nonverbal responses, such as eye contact, a nod, and so forth, are significant indicators of their attentiveness. Both their verbal and nonverbal responses need to be affirmed through your own words, eye contact, nods, and embracing gestures. These are significant features of acknowledging and encouraging children's participation. Yet they need to be offered in conjunction with a clear directedness toward consistent movement of the lesson along its intended path. If a child's comment indicates a direction off the focus of the lesson, it is important to redirect the focus as quickly and smoothly as possible, while at the same time embracing the child's participation.

Narrative:

Who knows what this is? *(Hold up the bellows.)* Some of you might have one at home if you have a fireplace or woodstove. It has kind of a funny name. It's called a bellows. You know what it does? Right, it blows air into the fireplace or woodstove. This helps you stir up a fire to warm your house. You see, the bellows helps the coals get plenty of air so that they glow and spark into flames. That helps the wood in the fireplace or woodstove to burn better and warm up the house more. We need that on these cold, winter-like days, don't we?

You know, we also need to warm up to God's love. That's what the season of Advent is all about. Advent is the time before Christmas. It is the time we have to get ready to celebrate Christmas and the birth of Jesus. Now, much of our getting ready has to do with things—decorating, cooking, buying, and so forth. But the most important part of getting ready, according to our Bible lesson today, is to grow in love.

God is like a bellows because God wants to stir up those embers of love in our hearts and bring them into a big flame that warms everyone. Some of you know the song, "Pass it On," that talks about sharing God's warm love. Isn't that a great song? Maybe it would be a good one to keep in our thoughts in the coming weeks, as we get ready for Christmas. Let's sing it together.

Prayer:

Let's pray. Dear God, we thank you for your love. We are glad that your love warms our hearts and helps us bring warmth to others. Help us in these days of Advent as we prepare to celebrate Christmas. Prepare our hearts with your love. Amen.

A PICTURE OF PEACE

Scripture:	Isaiah 11:6; Isaiah 65:25
Lectionary Day:	Second Sunday of Advent, Year A; Resurrection Sunday, Year A
Topic:	Justice; Loving Others; Peace
Illustration:	A picture, figurine, or banner featuring a lamb with a wolf or lion

Overview:

This lesson underscores the power of God's love to bring opposites, even enemies, into harmony. This harmony the Bible calls *shalom*, peace. It has a rich and comprehensive meaning in the biblical narrative. Isaiah presents one picture of that reality and hope in a vision that sets forth God's intention for people living together.

The prophetic picture is profound. On the surface the children will know what the picture is—a wolf or lion getting along with a lamb. But they, like many adults, will not realize the full impact of the picture unless it is explored, explained, and even "excavated" through the lesson. What something is and what it means are often different, especially in biblical symbolism. The lesson, then, seeks to probe the deeper meaning of the picture, that symbol of *shalom*, and to do so in a somewhat bite-size manner.

The picture, or figurine or banner, should be used to generate initial interest and discussion. Children may offer their perspectives on whether wolves or lions and sheep can get along. They may even attempt to suggest other animals. It may be important to give the children some latitude in discussing what they see and think regarding the picture. Yet the overall focus on teaching about getting along should not be lost in a discussion of the animal kingdom per se. It is important to bring the lesson to a focus on the question of how we as people, even though we are often very different from others, can get along with others. This is to be posed as a question and reinforced as a possibility in keeping with God's love and promise of peace for those practicing love.

Narrative:

What do you see (in this picture, figurine, or banner)? Do you think a wolf (or lion) can really get along with a lamb? They're not exactly natural friends, are they? In fact, they're kind of opposites, like enemies, aren't they? Can opposites get along? Today's Bible lesson says they can. And that God wants them to do so. Opposites, getting along—now that's a picture of peace!

It's hard to get along with some people, isn't it? Do you know some people who are hard to get along with? Yes, well, don't tell me their name! Can we try to love them? Sure we can! That's why Jesus came to earth: to teach us about God's love and to help us love others with God's love. As we get ready to celebrate Christmas and the birth of Jesus, it's a good time to remember how important it is to try to love others and make peace between people who aren't getting along very well.

Is it possible to be different, even when others aren't? Yes, I think so. That's why God gave us this great picture of peace. Can you imagine a wolf (or lion) and lamb being best friends? God can. That's peace. It's like opposites being drawn together. It means doing the things that make for peace. This week, as we get ready to celebrate the birth of Jesus, why not make a list of some of the things that make for peace with others? That way, we'll be ready to greet Jesus on Christmas Day and greet everyone every day.

Prayer:

Let's pray. Dear God, thank you for wolves, lions, and lambs, and all the wonderful animals you have created. Thank you for coming to earth in Jesus to teach about your love—love that helps us love and get along with everyone. Fill us with your love this Christmas, so that we can enjoy peace with people all around us. Amen.

LOVE-SHINE

Scripture:	Isaiah 9:2-7; Isaiah 61:10–62:3
Lectionary Day:	Christmas Eve/Christmas Day, Years A, B, C; First Sunday after Christmas, Year B
Topic:	Church Symbols; God's Light; Trusting God
Illustration:	Lighted candles (especially Advent candles, or other candles on the Communion table or other appropriate setting)

Overview:

Today's meditation seeks to connect God's light and love. Candles are highlighted as a symbol of God's presence and light. With God's presence, there is God's care. Thus, God is trustworthy. By highlighting the symbolism of candles, this invitation to trust God can be reinforced by the weekly presence of candlelight in the worship setting.

Point out the candles. If using Advent candles, you might comment briefly on their special use in the weeks before Christmas. Whether referring to Advent or regular candles, emphasize candlelight as a symbol of God's presence in Christ. In other words, candles remind us that God has come to earth in Jesus and is with us to help us. The initial conversation touches on the relationship of light and darkness in order to underscore the value of light. The focus is on the light and how even a small light can show through darkness. The concept of light and darkness as symbolic of good and evil, or comfort and challenge, is not one fully appreciated by children, though much more so by the adults in the congregation. Nevertheless, children understand the contrast between light and darkness, and this can be noted in highlighting the possibility of trusting God in our daily lives. Such trust means seeing and embracing the light more so than the darkness.

Narrative:

It gets dark early in December, doesn't it? That's why I'm glad we have special candles in our worship setting. Do you see them? (*Point them out.*) Candles remind us that God is light, and that God's light came to earth when Jesus was born.

So, even when it's dark outside, we can remember that God's light is with us. In Jesus there's no more darkness. Well, of course, we still see some darkness. Sometimes that can be a bit scary. Most of us are a little bit afraid of the dark. Even adults. But if we remember that God's light is with us, then we can scare the darkness away. Did you ever notice that even the smallest light can show through and break up the darkness? No matter how dark it is, even the smallest light still shows up.

That's why we have candles in our worship setting. The candles remind us of God's light and love. God is always with us, shining with love. We can trust God. So, we can make our way through any kind of darkness. That's important to remember every day. No matter where we go, or how dark it gets, God's light is with us. We can just pray and ask God to be close. The candles in our worship time remind us of that. And at Christmastime, especially, the candles remind us that Jesus brings God's light to be with us every day.

Prayer:

Let's pray. Dear God, we are glad that you are full of light and love. Thank you for sharing your light and love with us through Jesus. Help us trust you every day. Amen.

ON KEY WITH PRAISE

Scripture:	Psalm 96; Psalm 98; Psalm 149
Lectionary Day:	Christmas Day (or First Sunday after Christmas), Years A, B, C; Christmas Day (or First Sunday after Christmas), Year A; *(also Sixth Sunday of the Resurrection, Year B);* All Saints' Day or All Saints' Sunday, Year C
Topic:	Kindness; Joy; Praising God
Illustration:	Hymnbook (especially with notations of Christmas hymns)

Overview:

Most people, including children, love to sing Christmas carols. This lesson features Christmas music, with a focus on the role of praise in our everyday lives. If the church has sponsored a Christmas caroling adventure that children participate in, that can be noted in the course of the lesson. Or perhaps there is some other memorable songfest that could be cited in drawing attention to the participation of children and adults together in song.

The illustration for the lesson is a hymnbook or perhaps a Christmas carol book. In showing the hymnbook to the children, you cite something that is obvious to them. Then by talking about how we all are like hymnbooks, you draw out a completely new perspective for their consideration. In making that suggestion, you may sense a bit of bewilderment on their part. That's good. It means that you have their attention and can now talk more directly about the meaning of praising God and the role of praise in our everyday lives.

The point is to underscore the joy of praise through song and the foundation of praise in daily relationship with God. The lesson could be concluded by inviting the children to suggest a Christmas carol for the congregation to join in singing.

Narrative:

You all know what this is, don't you? (*Show hymnal.*) Right, it's a hymnbook (carol book). It's filled with songs we can sing to praise God with, isn't it? Did some of you participate in the recent Christmas caroling outing? (*Or ask if they plan to do some caroling, or phrase a similar question to get them thinking about their singing.*) Singing sure is fun. It's even more fun when there's a whole bunch of us together singing praise to God.

What's praise? (*Allow just a brief moment for children's responses.*) Yes, it means words of thanks and honor that we direct toward God. When we praise God, we say that we're glad that God loves us and we're thankful to be part of God's family. Except, we don't just say those things, do we? We sing them. That's what makes praise so much fun.

Well, did you know that we all are like hymnbooks? We can be filled with words of praise for God. I don't mean just by songs we sing. But also by how we live every day. Our lives can be filled with praise for God. Like a new song. Whenever we think about God, or thank God, we're acting like a book full of songs praising God.

Christmas carols tell us the Good News of God's love. They remind us of the special time when Jesus was born. And they encourage us to think about how special it was that Jesus came to live with us. That's why we praise God.

So, we are kind of like hymnbooks. I hope we're not off key! What do you suppose we'd sound like if we were on key with praise? Would we be filled with good words? How about loving and kind words toward others? Yes, I think so. Would we be careful not to get angry with others and say mean things? Right. We'd want to make sure we said good things to other people. That's a way we can praise God. And when we're here in worship together, we can sing the songs of praise with a special enthusiasm because we've been practicing praising God all week with how we live and speak to others.

Prayer:

Let's pray. Dear God, thank you for music and for giving us voices for singing. Help our lives to be like songs of love. Amen.

NEW CLOTHES

Scripture:	Colossians 3:12-17
Lectionary Day:	First Sunday after Christmas, Year C
Topic:	Loving Others; Christian Character
Illustration:	Old clothes; also a page of the words from Colossians 3:12b printed in bold, fancy letters, pasted on cardboard stock and taped or otherwise fastened like clothing to a clothes hanger

Overview:

Showing the children a handful of old clothes and making a joke about the clothes being new is the start for this meditation. The focus on clothing is in keeping with the apostle Paul's admonition about being clothed with compassion, kindness, and so forth. Again, like much of the symbolic language of the Bible, the point is to get our attention with something we know (in this case, clothing), and then move us to consider a deeper and more significant meaning in terms of how we think, feel, and act (in this case, the quality of our conduct).

In asking children about their new clothes, it is important to give ample opportunity for some of them to report and show off a bit. Yet at the same time, it is important to help them move from a focus on physical clothing to ethical clothing, as highlighted in the Scripture.

Narrative:

See what I got for Christmas? Do you like my new clothes? (*Point to old clothes.*) Oh, they're not very new, are they? I'm just kidding you. I didn't really get these old clothes for Christmas. Did any of you get some new clothes? (*Take a moment to let the children share something of their inventory of new clothes.*) Great! New clothes can be fun.

The Bible talks about putting on new clothes, did you know that? In today's Bible lesson, we're told to put on new clothes. But the Bible isn't talking here about clothing that we put on our bodies, but rather, on our hearts. Does that seem strange? Well, maybe. What the Bible is teaching us is that it doesn't really matter what we look like or what kind of clothes we wear. But it does matter how we act and live.

So, the Bible says we should clothe ourselves with good. We are to put on compassion, kindness, humility, gentleness, and patience. Wow! That's some outfit! Just imagine if everyone was wearing all these good things and sharing them with others. That would be a great world, wouldn't it? I bet we'd all look fabulous wearing outfits of love.

Well, just to remind us of how important it is to make sure we have plenty of compassion, kindness, humility, gentleness, and patience with us, I've made a special clothes hanger for you. You can take this home and put it in your closet. That way, every day when you get dressed, you can remember that

God wants us to be clothed with all kinds of special love for other people.

Prayer:

Let's pray. Dear God, thank you for your love. Help us each day to put on your love like clothing and to share your love with others. Amen.

THE NAME OF JESUS

Scripture:	Luke 2:21
Lectionary Day:	New Year's Day, Years A, B, C; (*also First Sunday after Christmas, Year B*)
Topic:	God's Will; Jesus' Name; Salvation
Illustration:	A "name book" (filled with names and their meanings) and/or a banner or sign with the name Jesus printed on it

Overview:

At the heart of the Christmas narratives in the Gospel accounts of both Matthew and Luke is the name of Jesus announced. This meditation focuses on the meaning of that name, with a view toward better understanding how the name reveals both God's character and intention. The point of the lesson is not to try to unpack all the theological significance of the name of Jesus, but rather, to underscore that God had a specific mission in mind for Jesus in choosing that name.

The lesson can begin by talking about names and then including a brief time to look through a book of names. This will give the children an opportunity to hear their name mentioned and maybe learn something about its original meaning. With limited time, it is best to consider a few of the children and their names beforehand. This way, you can concentrate on highlighting a few. Be careful not to overplay this, as frankly, some names are not particularly positive in their original meaning. For example, the common English name Mary, a variant of the Hebrew name Miriam, is rooted in the meaning of "bitter." When the etymology of a given name is not so positive, it is important to make a positive connection with the name. This can be done by citing important people, especially biblical ones, with that name. That, of course, would work nicely with Mary and other biblical names. This way, attention can be focused away, as appropriate, from the etymological meaning to a positive association for a name.

It may also be appropriate to offer to look up more names with the children at another time. Just be sure that you follow through on this and give them another occasion in the near future. An example of appropriate occasions for this might be a coffee/refreshment time following worship or during the Sunday school hour. This follow-up may help reinforce your connection with the children outside the worship setting.

Narrative:

How many of you have a name? Good, I'm glad you all do. How many of you got to pick out your name? Yeah, I guess you were all too young the day you were born. Me too. I probably wouldn't have picked my name. I might have chosen something else. Usually it's our parents who pick out a name they like and think would be good for us. After a while, we get used to them—I mean, our names. We may never get used to our parents, right? Just kidding.

You know, some names have special meanings. I have a book here with me today that lists all kinds of names and tells what they mean. Would you like to hear a few? (*Reinforce the sense that we only have time for a few right now, and mention looking up others later if you have a specific time to suggest.*) Well, did you know that my first name, ————, means "————"? Let's look up some of your names and see what they might mean. (*Take a few moments to look up some of the children's names, especially those that are particularly interesting or positive sounding. It's likely that time will not permit discussing everyone's name, so tell the children that we can look up some more another time. Just be sure you give them another occasion in which to do so, somewhat soon.)*

Well, wouldn't it be something if God picked out our name? You know, God did pick out the name of Jesus. That's what it says in our Bible lesson this morning. Even before Jesus was born, God had told Mary and Joseph that the new baby was to be named Jesus.

Jesus must be a special name, don't you think? Yes, it is. The name Jesus comes from the Hebrew language and means "God saves," or "God is our salvation," or "God is our savior." That's just what God said that Jesus would do—be our Savior. A savior is one who helps people and saves them from trouble. That's certainly an important name, isn't it?

When we say the name of Jesus, or sing about Jesus, we are reminded that God is our Savior. God offers us peace and protection. We can trust God. We can rely on God. That's reassuring, isn't it? By choosing the name Jesus, God reminds us that God loves us. So whenever we think of the name Jesus, we can remember that God is with us and that God loves us and helps us love each other.

Prayer:

Let's pray. We thank you, God, for sending Jesus to live with us on earth. We thank you for reminding us by the name of Jesus that you're our Savior, who wants to give us peace and protection. Thank you that we each have names. And thank you that we can call on your name and know you will respond in love to us. In the name of Jesus we pray. Amen.

EPIPHANY AND WINTER

BEING GOD'S LIGHT TO OTHERS

Scripture:	Isaiah 49:1-6; Isaiah 60:1-6; Isaiah 61:1-11
Lectionary Day:	Second Sunday after Epiphany, Year A; Epiphany, Years A, B, C; First Sunday after Epiphany, Year C
Topic:	Church Symbols; God's Light; Witnessing
Illustration:	Reference to the importance of light, illustrated by a lamp, a flashlight, or lights in the meeting place; the song "This Little Light of Mine" might also be used

Overview:

Each new day has a dawn. Dawn is the light that brings the new day. When Jesus came to earth, it was like the dawning of a new day. God gave us a new way to live—to live like Jesus did. This entails a new opportunity to learn about living with God and loving each other. Thus, every day is a new opportunity to walk in God's light and share God's love.

This emphasis on walking in light and sharing love is the focus of today's meditation. The lesson begins with reference to the illustration—any of a variety of light-producing items with which children would readily identify. A flashlight has the advantage of being mobile, and this may augment the illustrative point of bringing God's light to others.

Light, of course, is a central biblical symbol. In stressing this symbol of light, it is not to suggest to the children that darkness is bad, but rather, to highlight light as good. As they think about the power that light has to scatter darkness, so we wish them to understand the power that God's light has to bring good to people in our world.

Light, then, is a picture of God's goodness at work in the world. Children understand light in the physical sense, but the lesson at hand seeks to nurture an appreciation of light's spiritual nature as well. This entails making a connection between light and the presence of God in the world and the power of God to help us make a difference in our world. Focus on this connection is intended to help the children understand that they too have a role in bringing God's light, which is to say a sense of God's presence and love, to others on a day-to-day basis.

Narrative:

It gets dark early this time of year, doesn't it? During winter we may think more about how important light is, for we don't see the sun as much. But when the sun is bright during the day, it can pour right through a window and light up a whole room, can't it? And at night we have to turn on lights to be able to see.

You know, God wants us to be kind of like a window. For God wants us to let the light shine through us. What light? Well, God's light, of course. God wants us to be like a light to help others to see God.

Today's reading from Isaiah (which we have just read or are about to read) says that God's people are invited to be like lights in a dark world. Wherever there are problems and troubles in life, there is a kind of darkness. But God wants to bring light. So God asks people like us to bring light to the world. Every time we show love to someone, or help someone, or say a kind word, or share something we have with someone else, we're bringing light into the world.

We're being God's light for others. That's important, isn't it? I'm glad we have lights. And I'm glad that God invites us all to be lights for God. So, during some of these dark days of winter, remember that God wants you to shine like a beautiful light.

Prayer:

Let's pray. Thank you, God, for giving us light and inviting us to be like lights for others. Help us shine with your love every day. In Jesus' name. Amen.

GOD'S VOICE OF BLESSING

Scripture:	Psalm 29
Lectionary Day:	First Sunday after Epiphany, Years A, B, C; *(also Trinity Sunday, Year B)*
Topic:	God's Word; Seeking God; Worship
Illustration:	Reference to a storm, either a thunderstorm or snowstorm. Additional reference to the hymn "There Shall Be Showers of Blessing" is also possible. An object such as an umbrella or winter hat may also be utilized.

Overview:

The affirmation of this lesson is that God speaks, but we must listen if we are to hear God's voice. The picture presented in the psalm is that of God's dramatic voice of blessing. Through reference to the psalm and discussion of the different ways we can hear God's voice, the worship setting is underscored for children as an important environment for hearing God.

The meditation talks about God's voice, moving from the picture contained in Psalm 29 to the possibilities offered in weekly worship. Children understand about storms and may find them both adventuresome and awesome. In similar ways, listening for God's voice through worship includes adventure and awe. By underscoring the place of worship as a setting for hearing God, we invite children to become more active in their participation each week.

Narrative:

Have you ever been caught outside in a storm? Was it a thunderstorm or a snowstorm? Was it fun? Or a little scary? Today's reading from the Psalms (which we have just read or are about to read), describes a great storm. And in the storm, God's voice is said to sound like thunder as God draws near to the place where God's people are gathered. They have gathered to worship God, and they are listening for God's voice.

God is coming to be with them and to bless them. God blesses people by speaking to them and sharing love with them. God's voice is powerful, and in the psalm it sounds like a thunderstorm. Wow!

When we gather to worship each Sunday, we listen for God's voice too. Does God's voice always loud like a storm? Not always. The Bible also tells us that God can speak in a "still, small voice." And when we worship, we can listen for God's voice in various ways. We might listen for God while we sing loud songs. Or when we pray quietly. Or when someone reads the Scripture. Or when our Sunday school teacher or the minister talks. Or when we greet others with a handshake or a hug. We might even hear God speak in a smile!

The Bible reminds us that whenever God speaks, it's important to listen. It's great that we can get together each Sunday to hear God in so many exciting ways. And you know, throughout the week, when we smile and say nice things to others, they might just hear God speaking through us. Wow! Wouldn't that be exciting? Why not try it this week and see?

Prayer:

Let's pray. Thank you, God, for wanting to speak with us. Help us to listen and to share your word of love with others. Amen.

GOD'S TOOLBOX

Scripture:	1 Corinthians 12:1-11
Lectionary Day:	Second Sunday after Epiphany, Year C
Topic:	Church; Mission; Peacemaking; Sharing Talents
Illustration:	Carpenter's toolbox as an object lesson, with some opportunity for children to identify and comment on various tools and their functions, as time permits

Overview:

Affirming the equal value of people and their gifts is at the heart of this lesson, which draws from the apostle Paul's image of the church as the body of Christ. Helping children see that everyone has a contribution to make to God's family, and that God loves and blesses all people equally, is central to this understanding.

The lesson begins by surveying the diversity of tools in the toolbox. Since time is always of the essence, it is important to balance a healthy inquiry by the children into the kinds and functions of the tools with a focus on the larger message concerning gifts people have. That is, keep the discussion moving, so that it doesn't become bogged down in a preoccupation with the tools themselves.

Children certainly can understand how a carpenter's tools are used. The intent of the lesson is to build on this understanding by helping them to see that all God's people, even children, are like tools, gifted by God, to contribute special talents to God's people. These contributions as briefly illustrated in the life of the congregation can help reinforce the point.

Narrative:

What do I have today? Yes, a toolbox. What's in it? Tools, of course. Tools such as a carpenter might use to build special

things. Are all the tools the same? No. Let's look at some.
There's a hammer, a saw, a tape measure, a square, a wrench,
a screwdriver, a putty knife, a chisel, and so on. (*As time allows,
some discussion of the function of each tool may be engaged and illustrated.*)

We have many tools, but one toolbox. That's a lot like
God's family, the church. We're one people all together. But
we're all different. We all have different gifts and talents and
skills. We can do different things. Just like the tools. But
we're all part of God's family. Just like all the tools are parts
of the one toolbox. And we all have one purpose, just like the
tools. The tools work together to build something useful—
maybe a desk, or chair, or bookshelf. God wants us to work
together to build a world of love and peace. That's why God
gives every one of us special gifts and talents.

God gives each of us special abilities. Some people are
gifted in singing. Some in teaching. Some in building or organizing things. Some in helping people. Some in serving in
various ways. God gives us different talents, and God wants
us all to work together. Like one family—God's family. Like
the way all the tools in the toolbox work together to build
something special. God wants us to be building, too.

God wants us to build a world of love and peace. That's
why God has called us all together to be part of God's
team—a team of builders, a team of peacemakers, a team of
people who work for peace. Each of us has an important job
to do, for God has given all of us special talents to share with
each other. And God wants us to work together to share
God's love and peace with others. Now that's an exciting
project for us to do this week, isn't it? Let's ask God to help
us with the coming week.

Prayer:

Let's pray. Thank you, God, for making each one of us, and
for giving each of us special talents. Help us to work together,
to work for peace, as we share your love with others this
week. Amen.

GOD'S BANNER

Scripture:	Matthew 5:1-12 or Micah 4:1-5
Lectionary Day:	Fourth Sunday after Epiphany, Year A
Topic:	God's Will; Peace; Peacemaking
Illustration:	A banner with the word *shalom* printed in Hebrew; alternatively or additionally, a banner or sign with *shalom* printed in its English transliteration

Overview:

A large banner is a helpful feature of this meditation. It is especially nice if there are places within the worship setting where banners are or could be situated in full view as a decorative part of the worship environment. If a *shalom* banner could be visible for a number of weeks, it would lend a reinforcing element to this lesson. In this respect, it would serve to underscore the value of children's meditations that build upon each other, such that repetition and reinforcement are regular parts of worship from week to week.

This lesson focuses on the biblical meaning of the richly laden Hebrew word *shalom*. In addition, the lesson serves to teach children and remind adults that the Bible was written in languages other than, for example, English or Spanish. In acknowledging this fact, we remind ourselves as Christians that understanding the Bible involves a commitment to study the Bible—its language, history, culture, and message. At the same time that you try to help children understand this a bit, you are reminding adults, and indirectly encouraging them to consider renewing their own devotion to Bible study.

Narrative:

A lot of you kids go to school, right? How many of you are learning to read? Or already know how to read? Good. Well, today I brought something I'd like you to read. It's a banner, which is like a special sign. Who can tell me what it says?

(*Show the banner.*) Can anyone read it? I thought you told me you were learning to read. It's only one word. Take another look.

Well, you know, this word isn't as easy as it looks. It's not even English, is it? It's a Hebrew word, *shalom*. See, you read Hebrew this way. (*Show them how you read the letters right to left.*) It's one of the most important words in the Bible. It means peace, health, goodness, salvation, best wishes, and lots of good things.

Over and over again in the Bible this word *shalom* is used to describe what God wants more than anything in the world. But it's not an easy word to read and understand. We found that out this morning, didn't we? (*Nod in agreement with the children.*)

And *shalom*, peace, isn't easy to bring about in our world. There's a lot of fighting at times, isn't there? People don't always get along very well. Individuals, nations, and all kinds of people sometimes fight with each other and hurt each other. Fighting is the opposite of *shalom*. And it's *shalom* that God wants to see everyone enjoy in the world.

That's why God invites us to be part of an important mission in the world. God wants people who will help tell the world about *shalom*, about peace. And God is looking for people who will help show others what peace means.

Jesus says that such people are peacemakers. They are people who understand how important peace is to God, and how important it is to our world. Jesus invites all of us to be peacemakers—that is, people who help others understand *shalom*. We can do this by teaching others. And do you know how we teach others about peace? By loving them, being friends with them, and working to help people who have been hurt.

When we're trying to be peacemakers we're like signs of God's love in the world. It's like each one of us is a banner with the word *shalom* written all over us. We can speak *shalom* to others by everything we say and do. Now that's a pretty special banner, isn't it? A people banner! And Jesus says peacemakers will be blessed by God. Wow! Not only can we be part of God's plan to bring peace to the world, but also we can enjoy God's blessing. Sounds like a great opportunity. So, let's go in peace.

Prayer:

Let's pray. Thank you, God, for inviting us to be peacemakers with you. Help us this week to as we try to help others. Amen.

GOD'S SALTSHAKER

Scripture:	Matthew 5:13
Lectionary Day:	Fifth Sunday after Epiphany, Year A
Topic:	Discipleship; Helping Others; Justice; Mission
Illustration:	Salt, especially in a saltshaker; a further possibility is to bring and share some modest snack food, such as potato chips or pretzels, where salt is featured prominently.

Overview:

Today's lesson highlights another of the key symbols Jesus used in describing the role of God's people in the world. Salt is a common substance with which children are very familiar. Mission is the uncommon activity to which we as Christians are called. Using the common to illustrate the uncommon is what this meditation seeks to do.

The lesson begins with examination of the common element of salt, particularly in a saltshaker. Some time may be given to discussing with the children the uses of salt in our diet. They may wish to share something of their favorite foods and how they use salt. Amidst this discussion, you should move to comment on the importance of salt, especially in terms of its functions of seasoning, preserving, and healing.

Narrative:

Who can tell me what this is? (*Show saltshaker.*) Of course—it's a saltshaker. And what's in it? Yes, salt! Do some of you like salt? Yes, I do too. Salt is good with chips and pretzels and vegetables, isn't it? Salt adds flavor and taste. Salt can also help preserve foods so that they last longer. And you know what else? Salt can help heal. That's why when you have a cut on your leg or arm and then go to an ocean beach, the saltwater helps heal your cut.

Salt really is good—to add flavor, to preserve, and to help heal. And Jesus said that we are to be like salt. Does that seem strange? Well, Jesus knew how important salt was, and so Jesus was saying that we have important things to do in the world as followers of Jesus. We're to be like salt to help make the world a better place for everyone.

Now, salt isn't much good if it stays in the saltshaker, right? You have to sprinkle the salt around to have it work. So, too, for us to be salt like Jesus said, we have to spread ourselves around, kind of sprinkling goodness to others. Would you like to be like salt this week? Well, you can be salt, like Jesus said, by helping others and by helping heal people's hurts. We can help season the world with good deeds, kind words, and helpful hands. That certainly would make the world better, wouldn't it? That's just what Jesus had in mind, I think. So, let's see how salty we can be this week!

Prayer:

Let's pray. Dear God, we are so thankful that Jesus said we can be salt. We know that you have important things for us to do to try to help make the world better. Fill us with your goodness this week and help us to spread your goodness like salt everywhere we go. Amen.

GOD'S LIGHTHOUSE

Scripture:	Matthew 5:14-16 or Psalm 112:4-9
Lectionary Day:	Fifth Sunday after Epiphany, Year A
Topic:	Discipleship; Mission; Praising God
Illustration:	A lighthouse—either a model or picture of a lighthouse

Overview:

With many of the biblical images and symbols we encounter in Scripture, there is a need to "translate" them into understandable terms. This is true also of illustrations we use with children. In today's meditation, the symbol of a lighthouse may be a great way to try to translate the role of being a light in the world, as Jesus taught the first disciples. Of course, a lighthouse will be a clearer and more compelling image for those who live near coastal communities where lighthouses have served maritime travel for many generations. In circumstances where the lighthouse is not so familiar, its role may require an additional explanation.

The lesson, then, commences with a look at a lighthouse (in picture or model) and a discussion of the important role of a lighthouse for people traveling on the ocean. Once the image and function of a lighthouse are clear, the lesson can move to relate these to the commission of being a light in the world, as given by Jesus. Children certainly can understand the role of a lighthouse in helping people find their way safely along the water. Through the discussion of lighthouses, it is intended to help children see the importance of "being a light." This then sets the stage for briefly discussing ways in which we can be like lights—that is, being visible in helping others and showing them God's love.

Narrative:

Who knows what this is? (*Show picture or model of a lighthouse.*) Right, it's a lighthouse. Have you ever seen a lighthouse? I'm sure many of you have. Now, what do lighthouses do? That's right, they shine with a bright light, so that people traveling on the ocean can see the land and travel safely across the water. A lighthouse without a light wouldn't be much good, would it? The light is what lets the lighthouse point the way.

Jesus says that we're to be like lighthouses. Isn't that interesting? In today's Bible lesson, Jesus says that we are to be like lights in the world. What do you suppose Jesus means? (*Allow a very brief moment for responses, and then quickly focus the discussion again.*)

Jesus tells us to let our light shine before others, so that they may see our good works and give glory to God. That sounds pretty important, doesn't it? Yes, Jesus has a very important job for us to do. Just like a lighthouse, we are very important. We can shine and point people to God. That's how we do God's work in the world. God wants people to see us doing good things. That's how we shine.

What do you suppose are some of the good things we could do? (*Let the children have a brief moment to list a few things; be prepared with your own possibilities so to fill out the list and keep the message moving.*) Yes, we can help people in lots of ways. And do you know what else Jesus said? When we do good things, people will see us and then praise God. That's really important. So, let's all put our lights together this week and shine out brightly, just like a lighthouse, so that the good things we do will help other people, and so people will praise God.

Prayer:

Let's pray. O God, we are so excited about being your lights in the world. Fill us with your love, so that we can shine brightly and help people come to praise you. Thank you for giving us this important work. Amen.

GOD'S ROADMAP

Scripture:	Psalm 119:1-8; Psalm 119:33-40
Lectionary Day:	Sixth Sunday after Epiphany, Year A;
	Eighth Sunday after Epiphany, Year A
Topic:	Bible; God's Will; Seeking God
Illustration:	Roadmap, either as fold-up map or as
	part of an atlas

Overview:

Likening the Bible to a roadmap for life is the central theme for this meditation. Drawing from the image of Psalm 119, which speaks of God's word as a walk, a way, and a path to follow, this lesson seeks to nurture a sense among the children that reading, studying, and following the guidance of the Bible is a central feature of being part of God's family.

Begin the meditation with a discussion of what a roadmap is and does. Children understand something of following a map. Some of the children will have more experience with the use of a map. Some of their input can be elicited in listing some of the most significant features of using a map to find your way when traveling.

In discussing a map's function, a correlation is to be made with the Bible as a guide that, like a map, helps us find our way in life. It's God's directions to us to help us find our way, and know what's right and wrong, and which way to go as we make decisions and take actions.

Narrative:

Have any of you ever gotten lost? (*Acknowledge nods from the children, or mention something of your own experience getting lost.*) What if people have to drive to someplace they've never been before, and they don't know how to get there? What could they do? What could help them? (*Pause for a moment, and then produce the roadmap, either as a validation of the children's response or a prompt toward it.*)

Yes, a roadmap is very helpful. In fact, we might say it's necessary for traveling. A roadmap helps us get where we want to go. We can follow the directions in the roadmap and then find our way to the place we want to go. See, look here. (*Show part of the roadmap.*) If we want to go from here to there, we just follow this road as the map shows it.

The Bible is like a roadmap. The Bible gives us directions, just like a roadmap. It keeps us from getting lost by not knowing where we're going. Where does the Bible lead us? It leads us to God! The Bible helps us understand where God wants us to go, what God wants us to do, how God wants us to live. The Bible gives us directions. Today's Bible lesson talks about following the way God wants us to go in life. That means the way we should live, how we should act, what we should think is important, and how we should learn to live as God wants.

And what's more, the Bible tells us that following God's way of life is a source of happiness and delight. It makes us happy to learn from God. It's good to study the Bible, so that we can learn about God and learn to enjoy living like God wants us to live. Studying the Bible is like an adventure; it means finding out what's important to God and then following what God says. This way we learn about God and learn how to live happily with others. Now that's something to really be thankful for, don't you think?

Prayer:

Let's pray. Dear God, thank you for giving us your Word. Help us to study your Bible and learn how you want us to live. Teach us and delight us with your great love. Amen.

"Studying the Bible is like an adventure."

LENT AND HOLY WEEK

GOD'S GOOD NEWS

Scripture:	Matthew 4:12-25 or Mark 1:9-15 or Luke 4:42-44
Lectionary Day:	First Sunday in Lent, Year B
Topic:	God's Love; Good News; Jesus' Ministry
Illustration:	A newspaper, preferably with a large headline

Overview:

In this meditation, the emphasis is on how Jesus came to show us God's love, so that we could learn to love. Jesus taught about the Good News. Of course, Jesus didn't just tell about the Good News; he also demonstrated it. Central to the focus of this lesson, then, is an affirmation that God's word is an active one, and thus our response to it must not be confined to words but also must concern our conduct. The adults also may be reminded in this that the Good News comes to us and beckons us not only to declare that Good News to others, but also to demonstrate it through our total lives.

The newspaper provides a starting point for the meditation. Most children know what a newspaper is, and they understand that it has news of one sort or another. Looking at a newspaper, then, is a natural springboard to talking about God's Good News, which has come to us in Jesus. The children may have some opening comments on the newspaper, including mention of their favorite sections (if they are old enough to read parts). They may not respond immediately, especially if they are a younger group. In this case, mention a few sections from the newspaper, affirm their nods, and then continue. If some of the children do mention certain parts of the newspaper, then tie together a few of their suggestions and continue the lesson.

Moving from this opening conversation, you should identify the connection between the news of a newspaper and the
Good News of God. The concerns for justice, love, and
peace in the world are obvious connections. From here, you
can focus on God's news and talk about how Jesus embodies
the Good News of God's love.

Narrative:

Do you all know what this is? (*Show the newspaper, especially front
page, or another page with a large headline.*) Right, it's a newspaper.
Do you read the newspaper sometimes? What's your favorite
part? (*Allow a few moments for responses, and then move on.*) See this
big writing at the top. That's called the headline. It tells us
what the most important story in the newspaper is for today.

The Bible is like a newspaper, too. For the Bible tells us
God's story. And the biggest headline in God's story is what
we read (are reading) in today's Bible lesson: Jesus came with
Good News. Jesus told everyone the Good News that God
loves them. That's the big headline in the Bible: God's Good
News for us.

But Jesus didn't just tell people the Good News. Jesus
showed them. That was really Good News. We always learn
more by doing things, and not just talking about them, don't
you agree? That's how we learn: by both hearing and doing.

The people heard Jesus teach about love. But even more,
they saw how Jesus loved people. And Jesus asked them to
do the same: to love people. That's how we learn best, isn't
it? By hearing and seeing and doing. That's what God wants
us to do: hear about God's love from the Bible, see God's
love in other people, and then practice God's love by loving
others.

That's a big lesson, isn't it? During these special days of
Lent, it's a good lesson for us to be learning. A good lesson
about Good News. What could be better? Let's really work
hard in the coming weeks to learn how to be God's people of
love. I know that we can find some people who really need

that Good News. And we not only can tell them about it, we also can show them.

Prayer:

Let's pray. Dear God, thank you for sending Jesus to share your Good News with us. We are glad you love us so. Help us to share your Good News of love with others. Amen.

GROWIN' IN THE WIND

Scripture:	John 3:7-8; John 4:24
Lectionary Day:	Second Sunday in Lent, Year A; Third Sunday in Lent, Year A
Topic:	Christian Character; Holy Spirit
Illustration:	A fan, perhaps with pieces of paper or leaves to blow about to demonstrate how the fan can blow things around and move them from one place to another; use of the worship song "Spirit of the Living God"

Overview:

This meditation endeavors to nurture a working understanding of the Holy Spirit. It's a tall order, to be sure, but one that can be assisted with the use of a fan as an object lesson. If a fan is not available, a discussion of the wind, which children surely have felt and observed out of doors, could readily substitute. After an initial identification of the fan and its use, you may provide a brief demonstration of the fan's operation. Pieces of paper or leaves may help show that the fan can blow things around and move them from one place to another.

As part of this demonstration, you want to try to have the children focus on the "invisible" and wind-like nature of the fan. You might ask them if they can see the wind, or ask what color it is. Be prepared, of course, for less than empirical responses. You may well need to say for yourself, "I don't see any color, or anything."

Proceeding from the brief demonstration, liken God's Spirit to the wind and thus to the fan and its invisible power to move things. Herein, you wish to underscore that while we cannot see or feel the movement of God's Spirit, we can see the results of the Spirit's work in people's lives. This is just like seeing the paper or leaves move across the room. We cannot see the wind force moving them, but we can see the results. So it is with God's Spirit. We can see and experience the results in God's people.

You may wish to conclude this meditation with the use of the worship song "Spirit of the Living God" (or a similar song). As usual, be sure to have some key adults ready to join with you in leading the children and congregation in singing the song.

Narrative:

Do you know what this is? Right, it's a fan. A fan is a special appliance that can create some wind. You've all felt the wind outside, haven't you? Of course. Sometimes the wind blows gently, and sometimes really hard.

What color is the wind? What color is the wind that the fan makes? (*The children will likely look perplexed, shrug their shoulders, or perhaps answer that they don't know or can't see it.*) Well, I don't know either. We can't see the wind, can we? But we sure can see what it does. It can move these pieces of paper (or leaves) way across to there. (*Conduct your brief demonstration with the fan at this point.*)

That's just like God. God is Spirit, and spirit is like the wind. We can't see it, but we can see what it does. God works in people like the wind. We can't see God or God working. But we can see the results of what God does in people's lives. When God fills people with love and kindness and a concern for peace and justice, then we know that God's Spirit has been at work.

I bet that some of you know this song about God's Spirit moving in our hearts. It's called "Spirit of the Living God." Let's sing it together.

Prayer:

Let's pray. Thank you, God, for your loving Spirit, who moves in our hearts and helps us learn to live as your people—people of love and kindness and peace and justice. Move with us and within us this week. Amen.

Let's sing that song again as we move back to our seats.

GOD'S GLOBAL FAMILY

Scripture:	John 3:16
Lectionary Day:	Second Sunday in Lent, Year A
Topic:	Equality; God's Love; Mission
Illustration:	A globe or world map

Overview:

One of the Bible's best-known verses is the focus of this meditation. Familiarity can, of course, entice complacency with respect to Scripture. We come to know something so well that its impact is diminished. While this may true for the adults in the congregation concerning this verse, it is likely to be much less so, if at all, for the children at this point in their lives. The lesson, then, is an important one for them, even as it may serve as a helpful reminder to the adults in the congregation.

The meditation commences with a brief discussion of the globe (or map) as the point of illustration. For some children, the concept of the world and its many places and people is new. Some time may need to be devoted to help them understand that we are but a small part of the whole world. The lesson then seeks to move from a focus on the places of the world to the people of the world, and from there to God's love for all the people of the world.

Narrative:

Do you know what this is? Right, it's a globe (or a map). It's like a small model (picture) of the world. It shows all the different places in the world. (*Take a moment to point out and name some, perhaps one or two from each continent.*) Imagine all the different people who live all over the world.

The Bible tells us that God loves the whole world and all its people. All people of the world are precious to God. And God loves everyone the same. Everyone counts with God. God wants everyone to enjoy God's love. That's why God sent Jesus to the world, so that everyone could learn that God loves them, and so they could learn to love other people. Wouldn't the world be a great place if everyone shared God's love? When we share God's love, we treat each other with respect and kindness, don't we? That sounds like a great focus for this week.

Prayer:

Let's pray. Thank you, God, for loving everyone and for sending Jesus to help us learn how to love others also. Help us to think of others this week, and not just ourselves, so that we can learn to share your love. Amen.

PRAISING GOD

Scripture:	Psalm 95:1-7
Lectionary Day:	Third Sunday in Lent, Year A; (also Proper 29, Sunday between November 20 and 26 inclusive, Year C)
Topic:	Creation; Praising God; Worship
Illustration:	Hallelujah banner—a small banner with "Hallelujah" featured in colorful lettering

Overview:

This meditation seeks to nurture an appreciation of praise as an element of worship. The focus is the word "hallelujah" itself. Although occurring in many Christian hymns, it is not a word that is automatically understood by children (and by many adults). This lesson identifies the word's Hebrew origin and meaning, and then comments on its significance for our Christian understanding of praise and worship.

As a point of illustration, a small banner with the word "Hallelujah" featured in colorful lettering is appropriate. For an extra challenge, the letters can be rendered in Hebrew instead of English. But English is certainly okay, since the term is quite common in Christian hymnody, and the focus is on understanding what the term means for us, especially in relation to the joy of worship. If there are decorative banners in the worship setting, perhaps this banner may be added to the display. This would serve to reinforce the lesson in the weeks that follow.

Narrative:

Do you recognize this word? "Hallelujah." Does that sound like English? You're right; it's not really English. It's Hebrew, one of the oldest languages in the world. The word is from the Bible. It's the word that is used many times to talk about how to praise God. It's in some of the hymns we sing on Sundays, isn't it?

What does praise mean? What do you think? (*Give the children a few moments to answer, and then continue.*) Yes, to praise someone means to say something nice about someone. Do you like to be praised? Of course! Most of us do. We like people to say good things about us. We like people to appreciate us, and say kind things to us. We all need to be praised.

Why do you think we praise God? (*Give the children a few moments to answer, and then continue with a focus on why God is praiseworthy.*) Let's look at some reasons the Bible gives us. The Bible says that God is the Creator. This means that God made all the earth—all the beautiful places, plants, and animals. The Bible also says that God is our Maker. This means that God specially created each of us. And we are God's people. So God cares for us.

These are great reasons for praising God, don't you agree? And the Bible is filled with even more reasons. On Sundays we learn more about God and why God deserves our praise. That makes gathering in worship on Sundays very special.

Prayer:

Let's pray. Thank you, God, for creating the world and making each one of us. Thank you also for caring for us. We are glad to be able to praise you for your goodness. Amen.

DOING IT FOR LOVE

Scripture:	Matthew 21:1-11; Mark 11:1-11 or John 12:12-19; Luke 19:28-40
Lectionary Day:	Palm/Passion Sunday, Year A; Palm/Passion Sunday, Year B; Palm/Passion Sunday, Year C
Topic:	Church Symbols; Cross; God's Love; Jesus' Death
Illustration:	Palms (distributed during worship) and a cross (located in a central place)

Overview:

This meditation is designed for Palm/Passion Sunday. It seeks to address the dual themes of triumph and tragedy, victory and victimization, which bespeak the events surrounding the entry into Jerusalem and the beginning of Holy Week. There are two illustrative points of focus: palms and a cross. It is best that the palms be distributed ahead of time, probably during the opening of worship. It is assumed that there is a somewhat centrally located cross within the worship setting that can be recognized by the children and referenced during the lesson.

The intent is not only to highlight the difficult road Jesus chose to travel in expressing God's love, but also to note the possibilities for those who follow Jesus to be empowered by that love to do what may be difficult in their daily lives. In making the transition to highlight the cross, the lesson invites children to take inventory of some of the things in the worship setting. Only a few moments should be devoted to this part of the lesson, so as not to lose the focus. Direction should be made to the cross after a few moments of citing other things in the worship setting.

Narrative:

I see that some of you have your palm branches. It was great to see people waving them when we were singing the opening hymn. It's really nice to have something special, like palm branches, in our worship today, isn't it? Every time we have something special to add to our worship, it makes our time extra special.

But you know, there's something special that's always part of our worship. Every Sunday. Can you think of anything? (*Allow a moment for the children to cite a few things*). Yes, the windows, pews, pulpit, Communion table, organ (piano), the choir. (*Let the children briefly cite some other things.*) Yes, the people are here every Sunday. Well, of course, not all of them are here every Sunday! (*Scan the congregation as if looking to see who's there.*) But we sure couldn't have worship without people. But there's something else I'm thinking of. Something really important. (*If the children don't guess it by now, tell them*). Yes, I mean the cross. (*Point toward the cross.*)

The cross is the most important symbol we have in our worship. And not just for our worship, but for our lives. The cross means many things. It helps to teach us about God's love and how we should live. It reminds us that sometimes we have to do hard things, things we don't want to do. When Jesus came to Jerusalem, people were celebrating. Today, we've been celebrating too, waving our palm branches just like people did long ago. Yes, the people were excited. But Jesus knew something they didn't know. Jesus knew about the cross. Jesus knew that it meant death.

Now, Jesus didn't want to die. But Jesus wanted to show God's love to all the people. So Jesus came to Jerusalem to die. It was a very hard thing to do. Sometimes we have hard things to do. Oh, they're not as hard as what Jesus did. But they can be filled with the same love of Jesus. And someone else may benefit, just like we have from Jesus' love for us.

What if we were nice to someone who's been mean to us? That might be hard. But it would be great. Or maybe we could do something simple, like clean our room. Wow, that could be really hard! But if it helps someone else, it's great.

That's the cross. It means God's love. Even when it's hard to do something, we can do it out of love for someone else. That's what Jesus did. The cross reminds us of that. And it encourages us to keep trying to show love for others. I bet that Jesus' love can help each of us to do something this week that is really hard but really great.

Prayer:

Let's pray. Thank you, God, for the love Jesus gives us. Thank you for the cross, which reminds us that love can be hard to do sometimes. Help us this week to do the hard things that show your love to others. Amen.

THE TABLE OF JESUS

Scripture:	Matthew 26:26-29; Mark 14:22-25; Luke 22:14-20; 1 Corinthians 11:23-26
Lectionary Day:	Palm/Passion Sunday, Year A; Palm/Passion Sunday, Year B; Palm/Passion Sunday, Year C; Holy (Maundy) Thursday, Year A

Topic: Church Symbols; Communion; Jesus'
Presence

Illustration: The Communion table (with chalice and
paten, if possible)

Overview:

The Communion table and observance are a regular part of Christian worship, but are not always understood by children, especially younger ones. This meditation seeks to nurture an appreciation, in a modest way, of the significance of the table and observance for Christian worship. The table itself, along with the chalice (cup) and paten (plate), are sufficiently illustrative.

The meditation time begins by pointing out the Communion table and conversing about its place and meaning for worship. You may ask the children to relate what they know about the table and the observance associated with it, or you may proceed directly to give them an explanation. In either approach, the goal is to help them understand the historical background of the Last Supper in order to appreciate the Communion experience as a spiritual remembrance of it. In this way, the intent is to help the children understand that the observance is rooted in history and is shared as a remembrance by Christians all over the world.

Narrative:

Today we're going to talk about a table. (*Point to the Communion table.*) You've all seen this table before, right? Do you know what it's called? (*The children may or may not answer correctly; move quickly to give them the answer, if needed.*) It's the Communion table. I want to tell you about it.

But first, let me ask you something. Do you all have a table in your home? What do you use it for? (*Let the children have a brief moment to answer; as soon as one or two mention eating meals, proceed.*) A table is one of the most important items a family can have, because we use it for one of the most important things we do—eat food! And it's really special when we can gather around a table to share a nice meal with our family and friends, right?

Well, that's what Jesus did long ago. Jesus ate with people many times. Sharing a meal has always been a special way to share love with people. The most special meal Jesus ever shared is called the Last Supper. It's called that because it was the last supper Jesus had before he died. Jesus and the disciples ate together.

Now, when we gather around the Communion table during worship, we remember that special last supper that Jesus and the disciples shared. There was sadness in that meal because Jesus was about to die. When we observe Communion, we remember that sadness. But there was also some joy in that meal because Jesus loved all the disciples and Jesus came back to life to share that love with them again. We remember that joy, and we celebrate that love when we observe Communion together.

That's why the Communion table is so special. It helps us remember Jesus. It helps us remember how Jesus showed God's great love. And it helps us rejoice in sharing God's love with God's people. Sharing a little food and a lot of love is always something special.

Prayer:

Let's pray. Dear God, thank you for giving us food to share around our tables at home. Thank you also for giving us love to share around the Communion table when we worship. Feed us with your love, so that we can love others. In Jesus' name. Amen.

"When God fills people with love and kindness and a concern for peace and justice, then we know that God's Spirit has been at work."

RESURRECTION AND SPRING

SEEING JESUS

Scripture:	John 20:11-18
Lectionary Day:	Resurrection Sunday, Years A, B, C
Topic:	God's Family; Jesus' Presence; Resurrection
Illustration:	Church directory (or other collection of pictures of parishioners).

Overview:

Celebration of the presence of Jesus with God's people is the theme of this meditation. It begins with the resurrection story of Jesus appearing to Mary Magdalene, and it then describes how Jesus is present, and can be seen, in the people of God's family. The intent is to personalize the presence of Jesus and the possibilities of God's love in the people around us.

The mood of the occasion, and thus of this meditation, is celebrative. This is to be reflected in the use of the church directory (or other collection of pictures of parishioners). The intent is to celebrate Jesus, not as distant and abstract but as real and personal in the people gathered in the name of Jesus. The lesson attempts to connect the Pauline image of the body of Christ with the celebration of the resurrection event—the risen Christ amidst God's family.

The meditation begins with a brief recitation of the resurrection story as represented in the encounter between Jesus and Mary Magdalene. The "twist" in the lesson comes when, in the course of talking about "seeing Jesus," announcement is made about "having pictures." This then introduces the idea of encountering the risen Jesus in the lives of God's people. This concept, and the concrete pictorial, is likely to catch the children (and maybe the adults) a bit by surprise. This heightens the attention and excitement sufficiently to get the point across. The lesson should end on a joyful and celebrative note.

Narrative:

Today's a very special day, isn't it? (*Acknowledge the children's nods.*) Today we celebrate Jesus rising from the dead. Imagine that. Can you imagine being there early that morning when the big stone in front of the tomb was rolled away, and Jesus came back to life? Imagine seeing Jesus that morning. Would you have been surprised? I think so. Mary Magdalene sure was surprised. She was the first one to see Jesus alive again. And then she ran to tell everyone else that she had seen Jesus.

Wouldn't it be great if we could see Jesus today? Well, we can. I've got pictures! Really. (*Show outside cover of church directory.*) Jesus said that whenever two or three people are gathered in Jesus' name, then Jesus is there with them. Do we have two or three people here today? Look around and count. Yes, we sure do. That means Jesus is here.

So, how can we see Jesus? Look at this directory. (*Show directory opened.*) It's filled with pictures of people who believe in Jesus, who are part of God's family here in our church. So Jesus is here. And we can see Jesus in each person. Take a look around again. See the faces of all the people? That's what Jesus looks like today. Everyone who believes in Jesus represents Jesus to us. We see Jesus in each other. So, why not wave and say hello to Jesus in all the people you see here today? Now we can really celebrate Jesus being with us in the love we share with each other.

Prayer:

Let's pray. Dear God, thank you for raising Jesus to life. We are glad that Jesus is here with all of us as we share your love. Help us to treat each other the way we would want to treat Jesus. Be with us today and every day as we celebrate your love for us. Amen.

BELIEVING THE BIBLE

Scripture:	John 20:19-31
Lectionary Day:	Second Sunday of Resurrection, Years A, B, C
Topic:	Bible; Discipleship; God's Word
Illustration:	A Bible.

Overview:

Emphasis on the purpose of the Bible to teach us about God's love, especially as seen in Jesus, is the focus of this meditation. By believing the Bible's message about God, and by having faith in Jesus, we are promised life with God. This is an important affirmation toward developing an understanding of the importance of studying and applying Scripture.

The lesson begins with a look at the Bible itself. The children are familiar with the Bible, and especially Bible stories that they have encountered in Sunday school and other settings. This meditation builds on some of what they know about the Bible, but seeks to enhance their understanding by discussing something of the purpose, and not just the contents, of the Bible.

In beginning the meditation, you may ask them to mention some of the biblical stories, people, and events that they know. This may take a few moments, but is important toward underscoring their interest and involvement in knowing the Bible. From here, you can move to discussing the purpose of the Bible as indicated in the Scripture lesson for the day.

Narrative:

You all know that this is a Bible, right? Do you read and study the Bible in Sunday school and at home? (*Acknowledge nods.*) Tell me some of your favorite Bible stories and people. (*Let children relate some details; fill in other details as appropriate.*) One of my favorite people (stories, events, etc.) is ———.

(*Briefly share details.*) The Bible sure is an exciting book, don't you agree?

Why was the Bible written? (*Pause briefly for the children to respond, but then proceed quickly to answer the question.*) In today's lesson from the Bible, it says that one of the most important reasons the Bible was written is to tell us all about Jesus, so that we can have faith in Jesus. And if we have faith in Jesus, God gives us life.

Now, having faith in Jesus doesn't mean that we understand everything or don't have doubts about things from time to time. That's okay. We see lots of people in the Bible trying their best, sometimes doubting, sometimes making mistakes, and sometimes learning to trust and love God better. We can learn a lot from their stories and examples, can't we? We want to learn to have faith in God. Faith means that we trust God and want to live like Jesus. That's what gives us life in the way God intends it. The Bible is so important that sometimes we call it "the Word of God."

When we read and study the Bible, we can hear God speak in different ways. We can learn more about how to have faith in God and enjoy the life God wants for us. This means that the Bible is a real adventure. Let's remember that the next time we are reading the Bible. We never know what we might discover about God, and faith, and life. So let's keeping reading and studying and growing in God's life for us.

Prayer:

Let's pray. Dear God, thank you for giving us the Bible. We are happy to be able to hear the stories you want to tell us, so that we can learn to have faith. Be with us in the adventure of studying your Word, and teach us more about love and life. Amen.

UNITED FOR LIFE

Scripture: Psalm 133

Lectionary Day: Second Sunday of Resurrection, Year B
Topic: God's Family; Mission; Spiritual Growth
Illustration: Sports team picture (e.g., Little League or school or church sports team).

Overview:

Referencing Psalm 133's affirmation about unity, this meditation seeks to emphasize our life in Christ. The lesson advances that Christ has brought us together, unites us, and helps us live in harmony. Furthermore, Christ has overcome death and promised us true life with God forever. So, we should celebrate. The call to unity, then, is a celebration of the risen Christ.

The lesson begins with a viewing of a team picture from some sports activity. Personal anecdotes of sports participation may be added to the conversation with the children. These may be personal regarding yourself (as a player, coach, etc.) or concerning others among your family and friends. The point to underscore in the discussion of sports is the teamwork that makes sports activity rewarding. Moving from this affirmation of teamwork, a correlation to the nature of God's family can be made. Herein, you want to emphasize that since Jesus is our source of unity, following Jesus means enjoying each other's company and working together in carrying out God's will.

Narrative:

Today I brought a team picture from ———. Some of you play sports, don't you? Which sports do you like best? (*Allow a few moments for the children to offer suggestions.*) Well, in ——— and ——— (*name a couple of team sports*) it really takes a lot of people working together to play the game. You all know how important it is for everyone on a team to work together, don't you? When everyone unites and works together, a team can be a lot more successful and have a lot more fun.

Well, that's sort of like what the Bible says about God's people. All those who follow Jesus are like members of a team. We could call ourselves the "Church Team," I suppose. Maybe, there's a better name. What do you think? (*Give children a very brief moment to suggest something, and then proceed.*) Well, really our name is "Christian." That means we're all united by Jesus Christ. Jesus is like the captain of our team, who brings us all together as a team to enjoy life and share love with others.

I suppose we could say we're on "Team Jesus." And this means that everyone in the church is supposed to get along, work together, and enjoy each other's company. It doesn't mean that we always agree on everything, but it does mean that we all agree that we want to follow Jesus and do what God wants. We're united in trying to bring justice, love, and peace to the world. That's a big challenge, isn't it? So, we really do need to be united as a team. Okay, let's get going. (*It may be an extra gesture at this point to have an impromptu team cheer, if deemed appropriate: "One, two, three: team!"*)

Prayer:

Let's pray. Thank you, God, for inviting us to be part of your team. We are glad that Jesus lives with us. Help us work together this week to bring love and peace to our world. Amen.

LEADING IN LOVE

Scripture:	John 10:11-18 or Psalm 23
Lectionary Day:	Fourth Sunday of Resurrection, Years A, B, C
Topic:	God's Family; Jesus' Ministry
Illustration:	Stuffed animal sheep or lamb (or a figurine, a picture, perhaps a poster, or other representation of a sheep or lamb).

Overview:

This meditation seeks to highlight the biblical metaphor of God as shepherd and us as sheep. The Gospel of John passage and Psalm 23 both are relevant to the theme.

The lesson begins with identification of the stuffed animal. This sets the stage for discussing sheep, shepherds, and the biblical imagery. Depending on time constraints, you may have to decide whether to give greater emphasis to the role of the shepherd or the nature of sheep. To some extent, however, it is helpful to touch on both how God like a shepherd cares for us and how we as sheep need to stick together and rely on God.

Narrative:

Look what I have today. (*Show stuffed animal.*) What is it? Right, a sheep (lamb). Its name is ————. Do you like sheep? Yes, they're interesting animals.

Did you know that the Bible says we're like sheep? Does that seem a bit funny? Of course, we're not really sheep, are we? The Bible means that we sometimes act like sheep. Do you think that's a good thing or a bad thing? Well, maybe, it can be both.

Sometimes we just follow whatever we see other people doing. And we don't think for ourselves about whether what they're doing is right or wrong. Sheep do that a lot—just following each other without thinking about where they're going. That's not so good, is it? If we just follow along without thinking about what's right, we can get into some trouble.

But being like sheep can be good if it means that we stick together and follow what's right. And it can be great when we have God as our shepherd. The shepherd is the one who takes care of the sheep and leads them to good places to eat, get water, and be safe. When we follow God, we know that things will be all right.

In the Bible, God is described as our shepherd. And Jesus is said to be the Good Shepherd. That's something to celebrate. Jesus is the Good Shepherd, who loves us and cares for us. So, we can trust God and enjoy living together with God's people—just like sheep do.

Having God as our shepherd also means that we are to follow like sheep. Jesus wants to lead us in love, so we need to follow after Jesus by loving each other. So, let's stick together this week and follow our leader in love. That means everywhere we go, we follow Jesus' example of how to love others.

Prayer:

Let's pray. Dear God, we are glad that you care for us like a shepherd takes care of sheep. Lead us this week. When we feel like we might be lost, and don't know what to do, help us to remember Jesus. And give us the direction of your love through the example of Jesus. Amen.

KNOWING GOD

Scripture:	1 John 4:7-12
Lectionary Day:	Fifth Sunday of Resurrection, Year B
Topic:	God's Family; God's Love; Witnessing
Illustration:	Family tree or family album.

Overview:

Emphasis on knowing that we're part of God's family is central to this meditation. Focus is given to understanding that knowing God means loving God and loving God's people. This is an important connection in the link between theology (what we believe about God) and ethics (how we choose to live with others).

Spirituality in the Bible frequently underscores the inseparable connection between knowing God and loving others. In the Bible, knowledge is experiential and not merely abstract. Thus, knowledge is always linked to experience, responsiveness, and action. To know God is to respond to God, and, hence, to love God and to love others in keeping with God's will.

This lesson seeks to touch on this connection between knowledge and action by focusing on the concept of family. Children understand about family, even though the nature of their families may differ. In citing a family tree or family album as an illustration, the point is not to suggest a particular style of family, but rather, to present our relationship with God as being part of a family. In using this illustration about family, it may be important to move children through the sharing about family in a delicate fashion that affirms the various kinds of families represented in the discussion, all the while with the goal of helping them understand that they are blessed to be part of God's family.

Following the conversation surrounding our being part of a family, we can move to consider the way in which we are part of God's family. Herein, the connection between knowing God and loving others can be affirmed.

Narrative:

Have you ever seen a family tree (or family album)? This helps us see how a family is related. (*Show the family tree or album.*) We're all related to a number of people, aren't we? All the people we are related to are part of our family. We're all part of a family. Being part of a family is very special, isn't it? It means that we are connected to people who love us and care for us—people with whom we can work and play and share together.

The Bible says that we're part of God's family. We're all related by God's love. That's what makes us a family. As a family, we know God and love each other.

How do we know God? We know God through Jesus and the love that God shows through Jesus. By loving God's people, we show that we know God and love God. The Bible tells us that knowing God means loving others, and that loving others shows we know God. That's what it means to be part of God's family. So, we're like brothers and sisters together, aren't we? One big happy family? Well, we try! Have a great week in God's family.

Prayer:

Let's pray. Dear God, thank you so much for letting us be part of your family. Help us to really love each other and show that we know you. And help us to love other people and invite them to be part of your family. Amen.

THE ENDS OF THE EARTH

Scripture:	Acts 1:1-11
Lectionary Day:	Ascension Day (or Ascension Sunday), Years A, B, C
Topic:	Jesus' Presence; Mission
Illustration:	A globe (or large but manageable map in color).

Overview:

The doctrine of the Ascension is not the easiest in Christian tradition. But the truth that God has a mission for us throughout the world, and that God is with us in that mission wherever it takes us, is an important part of the meaning of the Ascension. This lesson seeks to underscore that God and God's people are present throughout the world. Identifying the "ends of the earth" with wherever we happen to be, and where God's people can go, is a modest step toward helping children understand that wherever we are or go, God wants us to bring the message and action of God's love to others.

The meditation begins with a look at a globe and some fun in attempting to identify the "ends of the earth." Moving to identify our own town as one end of the earth helps us see that God is with us wherever we are and wants us to carry forth the mission of love to others wherever we are. Moving from examination of the globe, the lesson underscores the view that God is with us, to help us love others, wherever we are.

This sense of understanding that God is with us wherever we go, and that God sends us to bring God's love to others, is a foundational point in developing a sense of commitment to world mission. Thought this lesson doesn't deal with world mission as a topic unto itself, it does undergird the basis for such mission.

Narrative:

Who knows what we've got this morning? Yes, the world. It's called a globe. The world is really bigger than this, right? Definitely! A globe is a model, a kind of round picture of the earth. Now, in our Bible reading this morning, Jesus said something about "the uttermost ends of the earth." Where's that? Can you find it on the globe? (*Let children look at the globe. They may point to certain places, like the North Pole, and you may note—and repeat for the adults—what they suggest.*)

In one way, the ends of the earth seem like places far away. Places where we aren't, or where we've never been. But in another way, the end of the earth could be anywhere. Could our town, ——— (*fill in name*), be the end of the earth? Well, yes. Jesus was saying that no matter where we go, even to the far parts of the world, God will be there. And even more, God will give us something to do: tell others about God's love.

So, wherever we are, God is with us. Wherever we go, God is already there. So, ——— (*name of your town*) really can be the end of the earth. And so can every other place. Jesus promises to go wherever we go, and to help us wherever we go to tell others about God's love. That's our mission. A mission is special work to do. Ours is to share God's love.

No matter where we travel, God is there with us. God has people everywhere, all over the world. So, we can be sure that God will be with us, to help us, no matter where we are or what we have to do.

God is like a travel agent who gives us plenty of love no matter where we go. And God wants us to share that love with other people every place we go. So, let's remember that this week, for all the places we go and all the people we meet.

Prayer:

Let's pray. Dear God, we are glad that you have sent your people of love all around the world. We are glad that you have promised to be with us wherever we go. Help us to always bring your love to others, no matter where we go. Amen.

COVERED WITH GOODNESS

Scripture:	1 Peter 4:8-14 (especially verse 8)
Lectionary Day:	Seventh Sunday of Resurrection, Year A
Topic:	Forgiveness; God's Love; Justice; Kindness; Sin
Illustration:	Jar of cheese sauce

Overview:

Central to this meditation is the emphasis on the power of God's love to overcome mistakes, failures, and problems we face in life. Children understand about making mistakes. They need to learn about the power of God's love and forgiveness in helping overcome failures and grow in love. This lesson seeks to help children understand a bit of how God's love helps us not only in doing good things, but also in overcoming bad things in our lives.

The lesson begins with a discussion of cooking and highlighting of the "all purpose" use of cheese sauce in making any meal just a bit better. From this conversation, you may direct the focus to the Scripture lesson from First Peter in underscoring the power of God's loving forgiveness. The point isn't to identify any particular sins or shortcomings, but rather, to uplift the power of love as a means of forgiveness from God and as a source of strength to overcome our mistakes. In this respect, it is important for children to know that personal failure is not "fatal" in our relationship with God. God's forgiveness can cover our mistakes and empower us to grow from our experiences.

Narrative:

Do any of you like to cook? What do you like to make? (*Allow a brief moment for the children to answer.*) I like to cook, too—sort of. Truth is, sometimes I'm not the best cook. But I have something that helps me make any meal a good one. Here it is. (*Show jar of cheese sauce.*) Do you know what it is? Yes, it's cheese sauce. Almost anything I cook tastes a little better with some of this cheese sauce on it. It's especially good for covering up some of the cooking mistakes I might make.

That's sort of what our Bible lesson today is talking about. Except it doesn't talk about using cheese sauce to cover up mistakes. It says that God's love can cover for our mistakes and failures. We don't always do everything just right. We make mistakes, don't we? We say or do things that hurt other people. We don't always do what's right, or fair, or just. But God still loves us and wants to help us make things right and do better next time.

But the Bible reminds us that God's love can overcome our mistakes. God doesn't forget us. God forgives us. And God invites us to keep growing in love. Love is very powerful. Like cheese sauce, it can make things better! Remember that this week, maybe when you're eating lunch sometime, or maybe when you've made a mistake. God's love can forgive us and keep us going and growing in love.

Prayer:

Let's pray. Thank you, dear God, for your wonderful love that helps us to overcome our mistakes. Feed us with your love this week, so that we may grow in our love for others,

and so we can better know how to do what's right and fair
and just. Amen.

"To know God
is to respond to God,
and, hence, to love God
and to love others
in keeping with God's will."

PENTECOST AND SUMMER

HAPPY BIRTHDAY, CHURCH

Scripture: Acts 2:1-21
Lectionary Day: Pentecost Sunday, Years A, B, C
Topics: Church; God's Family; Holy Spirit; Joy
Illustration: Birthday cake (decorated in red, orange, and yellow colors)

Overview:

Today's lesson features a focus on Pentecost as the church's birthday. Everyone likes a birthday celebration. By highlighting the coming of God's Spirit upon the first Christians, this meditation seeks to remind us of how God is always ready to give us the Spirit to help us live as God's people. This really is something to celebrate.

By pointing out the history of the church in "being born" in God's Spirit, the lesson endeavors to underscore the connection we Christians today have with all those who have gone before us. The day is a special day of celebration, and so the meditation time in featuring a cake should also be joyous.

It is good to be part of God's family. Thus, it should be a fun time for the children to celebrate. A helper to cut the cake and distribute pieces to the children is a must for this lesson.

Narrative:

Look what I have. (*Show birthday cake.*) You all know what this is, right? Yes, it's a birthday cake. Have you all had a birthday? And maybe some birthday cake? Of course you have. Now, whose birthday is it today? (*Be prepared for one child to mention someone in his or her family.*) Well, you know what? It's the church's birthday today.

Today is called Pentecost. It's the Sunday on which we remember the day that God created the church. No, I don't mean this building. I mean all the people who gathered in the name of Jesus many years ago. And here today we are gathered in Jesus' name just like they were. God started a new family in Jesus and we're part of that family, the church, today. So, we're celebrating the birthday of the church.

The church is many people. And so it's a big birthday party. Churches all over the world are celebrating today. Did you bring a present? (*Don't prompt the children to really answer this question; assume a negative reply and proceed with the lesson.*) That's okay. We all brought ourselves—that's the best gift anyone can give, right?

Some of you might know the hobbit story. When hobbits have birthdays, they give gifts to all the people who come to their birthday party. What a great idea! In some places in the world today, that's how people celebrate their birthday, by giving something special to other people in their family.

Well, that's just what happened on the day the church was born. In today's Bible lesson, we see that all the Christians were gathered together. And God brought the gift. It was a very special gift. It was the gift of God's own Spirit. There's nothing more special than you yourself.

When you give something of yourself, you are giving the very best gift of all. That's what God did. And that's what created the church. So, today we're glad.

Now, the church, God's family, is pretty old. It's had a lot of birthdays. But, you know, God's family is always new. Every time someone new gathers with us, it's like the church is new again. It's a new church. That's what God always wants—a new church, growing in love. God is always ready to give the Spirit to help us grow. That's why we're celebrating today.

So, let's sing happy birthday to God's church, and then have some cake!

Prayer:

Let's pray. Thank you, God, for this special day. Thank you for giving us the gift of yourself and all your love. Help us to share your love with each other, not just today as we celebrate, but every day as we live as part of your special family. Amen.

LIFE-GIVING WATER

Scripture:	John 7:37-39
Lectionary Day:	Pentecost Sunday, Year A
Topic:	Faith; Holy Spirit; Salvation; Spiritual Growth
Illustration:	Water can and a thimble (or other small container)

Overview:

Today's meditation is based on the words of Jesus concerning living water, faith, and God's Spirit. This is a somewhat symbolic and conceptual communication. The children may have some difficulty understanding it in symbolic terms. Although the symbol has common awareness (i.e., everyone drinks water), the symbol must be interpreted into language that has concrete meaning. If it remains conceptual, it remains detached. This is true for adults as well as children, but adults typically have more ability to make their own translation into the concrete.

The lesson, then, seeks to help the children understand the notion of filling up with God's truth. The drinking of water (which they understand) is likened to drinking from God's truth. What makes this possible is belief in Jesus. Thus, the role of faith is emphasized.

This lesson defers focus on the physical illustration until near the end. In this way, the illustration serves as a reinforcement to the message. Discussion begins around the message of Jesus and the symbolic action of drinking water, and then moves to underscore the role of faith in helping us to be open to filling up with God's truth. The different sizes in the water containers seeks to serve as a reminder that we have to make some choice and effort in augmenting our capacity for faith and being filled.

Narrative:

One day, Jesus was at the place of worship. While there, Jesus said to some people who had gathered around, "Let anyone who is thirsty come to me, and let the one who believes in me drink." People listened carefully. They weren't sure what Jesus meant. Jesus continued, "For out of the believer's heart shall flow rivers of living water."

What was Jesus talking about? (*Pause briefly, but don't expect or allow detailed responses at this point; keep the conversation unfolding.*) Jesus knew that everyone drinks water. We all need water, don't we? In fact, our bodies can't be healthy without drinking water regularly. So Jesus got everyone's attention by talking about something ordinary—drinking water.

But Jesus was really talking about something else. Jesus wasn't talking about being thirsty for water. Jesus was talking about being thirsty for God's truth. And Jesus was saying that those who believe in Jesus can drink of God's truth. That's an interesting picture, isn't it?

So now, who wants to fill up with the water from Jesus? (*Pause and proceed.*) Would you like a little or a lot of God's truth? Well, here. (*Show watering can and thimble, or other small container.*) Which of these will hold a lot of water? Right, this one. (*Point to watering can.*) Because it is so much larger.

So, if we want to fill up with God's truth, we need to open our hearts up real big. We want to hold as much as we can, right? If we get a lot of God's truth, we can share with others. Jesus said the living water of love will pour from our hearts to others who need love and refreshment. And there are lots of people in our world who need love, right?

So, let's open our hearts and listen for God's truth in the Bible readings and songs we have in worship. Then we can fill up with God's truth and love.

Prayer:

Let's pray. Dear God, thank you for promising to fill us up with your truth and love. Help us to believe in Jesus, so that we can be filled with your Spirit and can share with other people we see this week. Amen.

THE INVISIBLE COACH

Scripture:	John 16:4b-15; John 16:12-15
Lectionary Day:	Pentecost Sunday, Year B; Trinity Sunday, Year C
Topic:	Holy Spirit; Prayer; Spiritual Growth
Illustration:	Baseball cap

Overview:

Even though baseball is perhaps not the undisputed national pastime it once was, it is still a very familiar athletic activity. As such, it may offer a stepping-off point for talking about the role of coaching in sports. In this sense, other sports besides baseball would be equally relevant as illustrations. The intent is to describe the role of the Holy Spirit in terms of being a coach, albeit an invisible one. In this, the importance of counseling, encouragement, instruction, support, and leadership is briefly noted and underscored.

When I use baseball as an illustration, I make reference to my own longstanding involvement as a coach in Little League, as this helps connect my experience to the message. Such involvement, however, is not indispensable to the message, for the point is the nature of coaching, not one's personal experience.

Narrative:

I brought with me one of my favorite baseball caps today. (*Show hat; let children examine it and maybe try it on.*) Do some of you like baseball? I do. Do you like to play baseball with your friends? Are some of you old enough to be on a baseball team? Great!

Well, every baseball team needs a coach, doesn't it? A team needs a coach who can help all the players learn how to play, and help them play their best as a team. A coach is like a team leader, right? The coach teaches people on the team. If you want to play baseball, you have to learn how to throw the ball, catch the ball, and hit the ball. The coach helps you learn how to do those things well, so you can have fun. The coach organizes the team, to keep everyone working together. And the coach encourages all the players to do their best. The coach is very important.

Now, did you know that God is like an invisible coach? God's Spirit is with everyone on God's team—that's us. We're God's family, the church, God's team. Today's Bible lesson tells us that God's Spirit is with us. Jesus promised that God's Spirit would come to God's people to help them. And God's Spirit is like a coach who teaches and encourages us.

Every time we gather as God's family, we can be encouraged by God's Spirit, our invisible coach. God's Spirit coaches us in the Bible readings, the songs we sing, the fellowship we have with other Christians, and in the things we do to help other people. Wherever we are, all we have to do is think about God, and then God's Spirit is there to coach us, to help us with something we have to decide or something we need to do. And we can ask God's Spirit to coach us anytime; all we have to do is pray and ask for God's help. Let's ask God right now.

Prayer:

Let's pray. O God, thank you for being our coach in life. We are glad that your Spirit is always with us. Even though we cannot see you, we know that you are with us, to coach us, to teach us, and to encourage us. Help us to do our best in all that we do. Amen.

THREE-SIDED ONE

Scripture: Romans 5:1-11
Lectionary Day: Trinity Sunday, Year C
Topic: Holy Spirit; Trinity
Illustration: An equilateral triangle (either as an object or as a picture/poster)

Overview:

What could be more challenging to address with children than the doctrine of the Trinity? Since the doctrine is among the most conceptual, complex, and controversial in the history of Christian creed and tradition, and in light of the fact that the doctrine is not presented or defended as such in the Bible, it would no doubt be easy to choose not to address it, especially in a children's message. Yet the biblical message, as indicated in the Romans passage at hand, advances a threefold speaking of God and assumes such throughout the New Testament. Thus, it is important for children to begin to have an understanding of this threefold language of God, so that they do not come to think that such language refers to three different gods.

Clearly, the concept of God as Three-in-One is beyond human analysis and comprehension. The doctrine of the Trinity is but an attempt to describe the divine mystery. Today's lesson attempts a description as well. Without question, it is an oversimplified approach to liken God to an equilateral triangle. Yet the correlation may prove adequate in introducing children to the concept of God as Three-in-One as an explanation for the threefold language of God that they will encounter in the Scriptures.

The point of the lesson in making this analogy is not to minimize the complexities of the doctrine of the Trinity through oversimplification, but rather, to offer a picture that can serve as a starting point for understanding the language of the Bible and for appreciating the mysteries of God. In this respect, it is perhaps especially important for this lesson to proceed straightforwardly, without indulging too many of the children's tangents.

Narrative:

Who knows what this is? (*Show triangle.*) Right, it's a triangle. I bet that some of your older brothers and sisters study about triangles in their geometry math classes. And I bet that someday you're going to be a math whiz who knows all about triangles.

This is a very special kind of triangle. Like all triangles, it has three sides. But notice that all the sides are equal. (*Show triangle at different angles and let children visually measure it.*) The three sides, the three angles, and the three points of this triangle are all equal. (*Point to the sides, angles, and points.*) Each of the three is important to the triangle, isn't it?

If we took one side away, we wouldn't have a triangle. It would fall apart. We need all three connected. Together, all three make up the whole triangle. Each side contributes an important part of the whole. And so three parts make up the whole. It's one triangle, but with three important parts.

Well, you know, it's sort of like that with God. The Bible talks about God in three different ways. There's only one God, but there are three different ways to talk about God. Each way is important to our understanding of God. We learn about God in three different ways.

There's God our Creator, who gives us life and goodness. There's Jesus our Savior, who helps us receive God's love. And there's the Holy Spirit, who encourages us to share God's love with others. Each of these three is an expression of God. All together, this is who God is.

When we think of these three names of God, we can remember three very important things about God: (1) God made us; (2) God loves us; and (3) God wants us to love others.

When we remember these important things, then we're really putting it all together. Now that doesn't make us a math whiz, does it? But it does help us become more God-wise. And that's even more important.

Prayer:

Let's pray. Dear God, thank you for speaking to us in different ways. We are glad that you have made us, that you love us, and that you want us to love other people. Help us this week to remember your love while we study at school and do other important things. Amen.

BUILDING WITH GOD

Scripture:	Matthew 7:24-27
Lectionary Day:	Proper 4, Sunday between May 29 and June 4 inclusive (if after Trinity Sunday), Year A
Topic:	Obedience; Trusting God
Illustration:	Sand and rock

Overview:

Comparison and contrast are central to this children's meditation. The contrast is between that which is secure and stable and that which is not, illustrated by the difference between rock and sand. The comparison is between the stability of rock and God.

This lesson begins with an examination of the differences between rock and sand. In exploring the contrast, it will be evident to the children that sand is loose and rock is solid. This observation can then lead to discussion of which provides a more stable building surface, as suggested in the biblical story. A brief discussion of the need for a secure foundation in building may then be transitioned to a discussion of how God is a solid, secure, stable, and trustworthy foundation for our lives.

Following this brief conversation, the biblical story may be told. In many ways, the biblical story may stand in its own right in this meditation. The story clearly asserts the choice between a sure or insecure foundation. Once this distinction is underscored through use of the illustration and initial discussion, the story may well speak its word of invitation.

Since, like parables in general, the story is symbolic, it is helpful in telling the story to reinforce its meaning by inviting the children to consider how we can all better build our lives on God as our foundation. Giving accent to the wisdom of trusting and following God, the story carries a built-in invitation to trust and follow God with our lives. A simple stress of this point can help illuminate the message of the story and its implicit invitation. Sending the children forth with the thought of considering how we can build our lives on God, then, helps clarify that the story poses a question to us: How can we construct our lives in response to God's call?

Narrative:

Recognize these things? (*Show the sand and the rock.*) Which one is more solid? Right, the rock. Which would be more secure to stand on? Of course, the rock. I'm sure many of you have been to the beach and had your feet sink some into the sand. Sand isn't solid; it's loose and can move around. But rock is solid and makes a great foundation. You can build on rock. Houses need a solid foundation, don't they?

Well, you know, in the Bible, God is described as being a rock. Sometimes you hear God spoken of as "the rock of our salvation." And one hymn we sing calls God the "Rock of Ages." These are just ways of saying that God is secure, reliable, and can be trusted. We can trust God and build our lives on God. And that's really important to know.

Jesus told a story to encourage people to trust and follow God. Jesus said that everybody who hears God's words and acts on them will be like wise people who built their houses on solid rock. When the rain fell, and the floods came, and the winds blew, the houses did not fall, because they had a rock foundation. But everybody who hears God's words and does not act on them will be like foolish people who built their houses on sand. When the rain fell, and the floods came, and the winds blew, the houses fell with a great fall. They went "crash" because there was no solid foundation.

God is our foundation. We can safely build our lives on God. All we have to do is listen to God's word and follow what God says is the best way to live. Then we'll be really wise. Every time we study the Bible and try to do what God wants, we are learning to trust God and be wise. And that's the best foundation for living there can be.

Prayer:

Let's pray. Dear God, thank you for sand and beaches, and for rocks and houses. And thank you for teaching us how to build our lives on you. Help us to trust and follow you more each day. Amen.

TENTING WITH GOD

Scripture:	Psalm 46:1-7; Psalm 18:1-3 or Psalm 91:1-6
Lectionary Day:	Proper 5, Sunday between June 12 and 18 inclusive (if after Trinity Sunday), Years A, B; Proper 7, Sunday between June 19 and 25 inclusive, Year A
Topic:	Creation; Faith; God's Protection; Trusting God
Illustration:	Camping tent (or a picture of one)

Overview:

The book of Psalms is filled with pictures of God's care and protection. Pictures of God as a refuge, a shelter, a tent, a rock, a stronghold, a fortress, and a shield all affirm God's strength and reliability. This lesson focuses on one picture: a tent. The tent bespeaks a tenet. The tenet of faith is clear: With God, we can trust and be safe.

This lesson centers on divine providence and protection. The tent is used as an example of a protective shelter. The notion of God as a protective shelter for our lives, then, may come a bit more to life through this illustration.

The message begins with focus on the illustration of a tent. It's important to devote a good bit of time for the children to discuss the use and function of a tent in the camping experience. Amidst this discussion, affirmation of a tent's role in providing protective shelter is important. From that point, the discussion may proceed to an affirmation of God's promise of protection.

Through the illustration and discussion, then, it is hoped that children will catch a glimpse of the trustworthy nature of God, and be encouraged to trust more in God's love and protection in their lives. This then becomes a tenet of faith—that God is a ready source of strength and help for us in meeting the challenges of life.

Narrative:

How many of you have ever been camping? Great! I love camping. It's great to be outdoors and enjoy all the beautiful trees, plants, and flowers that God has made. Don't you agree? (*Acknowledge the children's nods.*) What are some of the places you've been camping in? (*Give the children a few moments to recite some of their experiences.*)

Did you sleep outside in a tent? (*Acknowledge their responses, and then proceed.*) Tents are a lot of fun, aren't they? Tents are also very important for protection. You know, I've slept outside in a tent when it's been raining, and snowing, and cold.

Without a tent, I would have been wet, cold, and miserable. But with my tent, I stayed dry, warm, and had a great time.

Tents are a very special kind of shelter and protection, aren't they? You can take a tent almost anywhere, so that you can be protected from the rain and snow and cold.

Well, did you know that the Bible refers to God as a special kind of shelter and protection? In a sense, God is like a very special kind of tent. Like a tent, God goes anywhere with us. And God promises to care for us and help us.

Now, that's exciting, isn't it? We can trust God because God loves us. And with God's help, we can love each other.

Prayer:

Let's pray. Dear God, thank you that we can talk with you and trust you. We are glad that you are like a special shelter for us. Thank you for loving us and caring for us. Help us to love and care for others this week. Amen.

STOP FIGHTING

Scripture:	Psalm 46:7-11
Lectionary Day:	Proper 6, Sunday between June 12 and 18 inclusive (if after Trinity Sunday), Years A, B
Topic:	God's Will; Peace; Sin
Illustration:	War toys (plastic figures, video games, or pictures of them, perhaps from an advertising flyer that highlights a variety of such fighting toys)

Overview:

This meditation concerns linking the knowledge of God with the commitment to peace. In Psalm 46, the Hebrew word behind the common translation "be still" carries in the context of the psalm the sense of "stop fighting." According to the biblical psalmist, then, as well as many of the prophets, to know God means to cease and desist from violence, that is, to stop fighting.

This assertion is central to this psalm and meditation. The theological component to this assertion is that peace is central to God's nature and intention. The ethical component is that peacemaking is central to God's will and calling for God's people. Hate and hostility are incompatible with the love and life that characterize our relationship with God.

This message, then, confronts head-on the violent world in which we live, and the rather militant culture in which many of our children are nurtured. The overabundance of violent television shows, videos, and games has certainly contributed to a widespread desensitizing to the evil effects of violence, especially among children, who are very vulnerable to the violence-saturated images of the media and toy market.

The example of a few war toys (plastic figures, video games, or pictures of them) serves as a starting point for the lesson. This illustration should be referenced quickly. It is important not to get caught up in a discussion of toys in general, or war-related ones in particular. The illustration is just a starting point for the discussion.

The emphasis is on peace. The focus is God's call for us to stop fighting, be still, listen to God, and see that God wants us to be people of peace.

Narrative:

Shhh … (*Show finger to lips gesture as a signal for quiet.*) Let's be real quiet for a moment. In today's Bible lesson, God tells us to be quiet and to stop fighting and to know God. We all want to know God, right? So, we need to listen when God speaks to us.

Sometimes it's hard to listen, though, isn't it? Some things distract us, and keep us from hearing God. Here are some things. (*Point to war toys or pictures of them.*) These are some fighting toys, aren't they? Do you suppose God wants us to learn about fighting and war?

No, I don't think so. I think God wants us to learn about justice, love, and peace.

In today's Bible reading, it says that God wants to destroy all fighting things and to stop all wars. God wants us to stop for a moment, be still, listen, and hear God, so that we can know God better. If we stop fighting, we can pay attention to God and know God. And if we know God, then we'll know what God wants in the world, and what we're supposed to do.

God wants peace in the world. God wants us to learn about peace and to practice peace. Too often we learn about fighting, and practice fighting, even if it's only pretend. But God wants peace rather than fighting.

If we're going to pretend, why don't we pretend that the world is full of peace and the knowledge of God? Wouldn't that be great! Peace is what God wants. If we pretend peace, maybe it will lead us to practice peace. What do you think?

Then we can know God better. And we can be the people of peace that God wants us to be. So let's try to listen to God's voice of peace this week.

Prayer:

Let's pray. Dear God, we know that you want peace for all us, but our world is so filled with fighting. Help us to listen to you, and help us to choose peace instead of fighting. Thank you that you are our God, and that we can know you. Amen.

THIRSTY FOR GOD'S LOVE

Scripture:	Psalm 42:1
Lectionary Day:	Proper 6, Sunday between June 12 and 18 inclusive (if after Trinity Sunday), Year C
Topic:	God's Love; Seeking God; Spiritual Growth

Illustration: A picture, figurine, or model of a deer,
                   along with some water, perhaps in a
                   pitcher with small paper cups to distrib-
                   ute to the children who might like to try
                   a small drink during the lesson time

Overview:

Everyone knows what it's like to be thirsty. Following the
image offered by the psalmist, this meditation compares the
desire to have a drink to quench our thirst with the seeking
after God to fulfill our spirits. In a sense, the meditation re-
flects something of the prayerful assertion attributed to St.
Augustine: "O God, our souls are restless until they rest in
you." The desire for God is at one with our need for love,
and in our yearning we may find both.

The meditation focuses on the image of the psalmist in
which seeking God is likened to a deer seeking water. This is
a powerful picture and requires little interpretation. Children
will readily recognize the need for water, and will understand
a deer seeking to quench its thirst at a stream.

The key to the lesson is in connecting this very ordinary
matter—thirst—with the more extraordinary longing for
God. Herein, the concept of being thirsty for God is introduced.

Narrative:

Have you ever seen a deer? (*Show picture or figurine.*) They certainly are beautiful creatures, aren't they? And they know how
to find water to drink, at a stream or by a lake. They know
how important it is to drink water regularly, and sometimes
they will travel quite a distance to get a drink.

Do you get very thirsty sometimes, especially during hot
summer days? Yes, I bet you do. It's important for all of us to
drink plenty of water. Our bodies need a good watering every
day, don't they? (*Don't pause but nod affirmatively and keep the conversation unfolding.*)

Can we be thirsty for God? Yes, I think we can. If we're thirsty for God, it means that we desire to know God, we seek to follow God, and we long to be with God. That's what the Bible lesson means when it says, "As a deer longs for flowing streams, so my soul longs for you, O God. My soul thirsts for God, for the living God." Being thirsty for God means that we want to know God better and enjoy God's love.

Well, you know, we can drink of God's love every Sunday when we gather to worship God and be with God's family. And we can drink of God's love every day, and we can share that love with others who are thirsty. Everyone's thirsty for love, don't you think? Yes, indeed.

So, remember this week, every time you have a drink of water, that when we are thirsty for God, we want to be filled with God's love, so that we can share that love with others.

Prayer:

Let's pray. Thank you, God, for creating beautiful animals, like deer. Thank you also for loving us. Make us thirsty for your love, so that we seek you always, and always seek to share your love with other people. Amen.

GOD'S RECIPE FOR GOODNESS

Scripture:	Galatians 5:22-25
Lectionary Day:	Proper 8, Sunday between June 26 and July 2 inclusive, Year C
Topic:	Christian Character; Discipleship; Holy Spirit; Peace
Illustration:	Galatians 5:22-23a printed out in bold and colorful lettering on an 8½-by-11-inch sheet of paper; can or jar of fruit cocktail; alternatively, have a basket of fresh fruit (with enough variety so as to

be able to emphasize the mixing together
of good ingredients)

Overview:

This meditation is designed for a Sunday following Pentecost.
It seeks to highlight the variety of goodness that God wants
to nurture in each of us. It stresses virtue as a variety of
goodness. In this, the lesson underscores key qualities of
Christian character, with emphasis on the attitudes and actions that bespeak character in keeping with God's goodness.

The meditation begins with soliciting a list of favorite
foods from the children. After a few moments, the can or jar
of fruit cocktail is introduced and described. The fruit cocktail, with its mixture of fruit, then sets the stage for referencing the Scripture from Galatians and talking about the various
ingredients in God's menu for our lives.

Narrative:

Who has a favorite food? What kind? (*Let the children respond.*)
Great! Oh, I like that too. Well, here's something. (*Show the
container of fruit cocktail.*) Do you know what this is? Sure, it's
fruit cocktail. What's fruit cocktail? Yes, it's a whole bunch of
good fruit mixed together. It's really good food for us, isn't
it? Because it has such a variety of good things in all the different fruit.

Did you know that God has a special kind of fruit cocktail
for Christians? Yes, today's Scripture lesson today is about
fruit cocktail! Well, sort of. It's about what's called the "fruit
of the Spirit." It includes all the good qualities that God
wishes for us as people.

The fruit of the Spirit includes all the good things God
gives. It's like fruit cocktail. It's all the goodness that God
wants to put into all of us.

We're like fruit cocktail. Does that mean God wants us to
be fruity people? Well, maybe not. But it does mean God
wants us to grow in all the different ways of God's goodness.

That's what the Bible means by the fruit of the Spirit—the many good qualities that God shares with us. It means that we can have God's goodness.

God has a recipe for goodness. It includes love, joy, peace, patience, and kindness. These are the things that God wants us to think about and do. Like fruit cocktail, it's a lot of good things all together. One of those is peace. Peace is an important work of God's Spirit in our lives. And peace is all mixed together with love and kindness and gentleness and so forth, just like all the good fruit is mixed together in a container of fruit cocktail.

Now, wouldn't you say we could use a lot more peace in our world? We hear a lot about people fighting and hurting each other, don't we? Sometimes we're tempted to fight with people. Sometimes we fight with words, don't we? Like when we say mean things to someone. But you know, the more we partake of God's goodness, the more we can stay away from fighting and be nice to others instead.

Wouldn't it be a great world if everyone and every country did that? Just imagine how good the world could be if we were kind and patient with other people. That really would be good, wouldn't it?

Well, you know, that's what God wants. The fruit of the Spirit is God's health food for all us. It's good food for our spirits. So, let's all eat hearty this week, with good helpings of peace and love and kindness that we can share with others. And who knows, maybe the whole world will get just a little bit fruitier—and a whole lot better.

Now here, I have something for you. (*Hand out the "fruit of the Spirit" sheet*). This is for your refrigerator at home. Put it right on the door. Every time you open the refrigerator to get something to eat, you can see God's recipe for us. That way, every time we get something to eat and put inside our bodies, we can remember what God wants to put in hearts and lives.

So here's your recipe. It's filled with good things all mixed together, just like fruit cocktail. You can't pick and choose, now. We need all of this together: love, joy, peace, patience, kindness, and the rest. God wants to feed us these good things. And you know what? With these things, you can never overeat. Because these are things you can never get too much of. So, eat hearty!

Prayer:

Let's pray. Thank you, God, for giving us good food for our bodies and spirits. Thank you for your recipe for goodness. We are glad that you have so many good things to give us to help us live and love others. Feed our hearts and minds with your peace, that we may live in peace with everyone. Feed us this week with your love, peace, and kindness, so that we may grow and be your healthy and helpful people. Amen.

GROWING WITH GOD (OR, GOD'S GARDEN)

Scripture:	Matthew 13:1-9,18-23 or Mark 4:1-9,13-20 or Luke 8:4-8,11-15
Lectionary Day:	Proper 10, Year A
Topic:	God's Word; Obedience; Spiritual Growth
Illustration:	Two containers: one filled with potting soil and one with rocks

Overview:

A distinction between listening to and ignoring God's word is at the heart of this meditation. Focus is on the receptivity required of people in receiving and responding to what God teaches and seeks to do in our lives.

The illustration is based on the parable of the sower, and it underscores the difference in the kinds of soil. It is obvious to everyone, including the children, that the good soil is better for growing things. The lesson, then, seeks to highlight Jesus' illustration about good receptivity bringing forth a good response. In discussing the difference between the soils, and how important good soil is to growing things, it is helpful to make gardening a bit personal by mentioning your own experience or that of another close to you (e.g., my grandfather, in my case).

Planting time is an obvious occasion for this. In posing the choice between the two kinds of soil being illustrated, the point is to remind us that we often have to make choices to pay attention, hear God's Word, and then try to live it out. Since both children and adults understand about growing, we can also understand something of what it takes to allow God's word and love to grow in us.

By visualizing ourselves as gardens, we can help focus on what our lives are producing by way of good growth. This is an image that may well stay with children throughout the summer every time they see things growing in flower and vegetable gardens.

Narrative:

Do you like stories? I know you do. I do, too. Most people do. Jesus told a lot of stories to people. By telling stories, Jesus taught people about God and about how they should live.

In today's Bible lesson, we heard (or will hear) about a story Jesus told. In the story, Jesus said that people are kind of like dirt. Now, Jesus wasn't trying to insult anyone. Jesus was just saying that people are like gardens that grow things.

Now, which of these do you think is better for growing things? (*Show the two kinds of soil.*) Yes, I agree, this one looks much better. What's the matter with this other one? Right, it doesn't have enough good soil.

You know, my grandfather always told me that good soil is the key to a good garden. If you want to grow good things in your garden, you have to have good soil.

That's what Jesus was talking about. Jesus went around teaching people about God's love. Jesus was like a farmer trying to plant God's word and love in people's lives. But whether anything would grow depended on the people. What kind of soil did they have for God's word?

You see, things grow inside and outside of us. Some things are good, like love and kindness. But some things aren't so good, like hate and meanness. Jesus wants to plant good things in our lives. Good things like peace and justice for others.

Now then, what kind of soil do we want to be? Don't we want to be good soil like this (*point to potting soil*), so that good things from God can grow in us? Sure we do. Something's always growing. We just need to pay attention to what God teaches us, so that good things can grow. We want good things to grow out of our hearts and lives.

That's why when we gather together each Sunday we try to listen to the Bible being read, so we can know how to grow good things, like love, in our lives. And of course, God is always there to help us.

But watch out for the weeds! Sometimes we feel like being grumpy or mean. That's when some of those rocks (*point to rocks*) get into our gardens. And then weeds grow, instead of beautiful things like flowers. When we listen to God's word, we let beautiful things like love grow.

All of you are growing children. But you know, even we adults need to keep growing in God's love. So, let's all work together and help each other to grow love in our lives.

Prayer:

Let's pray. Dear God, it is so nice to be able to be part of your garden of love. Help us to listen to your word and be able to grow good things, like love, in our lives. Thank you for giving us good stories to learn and live by. In Jesus' name we pray. Amen.

SEEING THE FRUIT IN THE SEED

Scripture:	Matthew 13:31-32; Mark 4:30-32; *alternatively, Luke 13:18-19*
Lectionary Day:	Proper 6, Sunday between June 19 and 25 inclusive, Year B; Proper 11, Sunday between July 17 and 23 inclusive, Year A
Topic:	Christian Character; Creation; Potential; Spiritual Growth
Illustration:	A handful of seeds (e.g., apple seeds)

Overview:

At the heart of this meditation is a focus on the purpose and potential implicit in the reign (kingdom) of God. Understanding the potential that God sets forth for us as people, in response to that reign, is the key. Herein, the ordinary becomes the extraordinary. This is rooted in our reflection on the power of potential that is packaged, as it were, like a seed, which carries within all the promise of fruit and fulfillment.

The lesson commences with the illustration of seeds and a discussion of how seeds can grow into fruit. The message is pinpointed in this simple observation: tiny seeds may grow into great trees and bear rich fruit. In a similar manner, God works in the world and in each of our lives. God's reign unfolds in the attitudes and actions of love and justice that we express.

Jesus originally told the brief parable in the Gospel passage at a point when people doubted, or at least questioned, how the mighty power of God's reign could be associated with the rather mundane ministry of Jesus and the disciples about the countryside of Galilee. Why hadn't God's kingdom come with explosive and irresistible power, as many thought it would? Instead, as Jesus suggested in the parable, God's reign has burst forth in seed-like form. Yet it arrives with all the potential, promise, and power of God's love. People, therefore, ought not be dismayed by its small beginnings, but rather, determined to embrace its sure potential.

A small "growing project" might also be arranged and combined with this lesson. Small containers with soil and ready for planting could be prepared ahead of time. Then flower, or perhaps vegetable, seeds could be provided for children to plant. Assuming that the physical environment of the worship setting would be suitable for plant growth (with adequate natural light, etc.), the containers could be arranged throughout the worship setting. The sprouting and growth of the seeds in the coming weeks would then present an ongoing reiteration and continuation of the message.

Narrative:

Do you know what these are? Sure, they're seeds. What kind? Yes, they're from an apple (or other) tree. Now, do you know what they might be someday? That's right—apples. And maybe even apple pie!

Let's imagine for a moment. Close your eyes. Remember the seeds we've just looked at. Now think about those seeds growing into apples. Picture delicious apples filling out an apple tree. Wow, what a sight! It's making me hungry just thinking about those great apples.

But are we just pretending? Well, not really. These seeds are real, aren't they? They're not pretend. Each seed has all the potential of a full-grown, delicious apple. God puts all the potential of full-grown fruit into every seed.

In one sense, it's ordinary, but in another sense it's really extraordinary, isn't it? That's one of the everyday miracles. It's something to think about every time we eat some good fruit, right?

But there's something else to think about, too. Did you know that God puts a whole bunch of potential in every person? And God sees that potential from the day we're born. God plants seeds of love and peace in all of us. And God wants those seeds of love and peace to grow. That's the potential God puts in all of us.

We might not know where we'll be, or what we'll be doing when we get older. But God sees the potential in us right now. And wherever we go, and whatever we do, God knows that if we take care of the seed that God has planted in us, it will grow and grow, and become wonderful.

Just think, if we all let the seeds of love and peace grow in our hearts and in our actions each day, what a better world it would be—a world with all the potential that God sees in each of us. Then God's love could really reign all over the world.

Prayer:

Let's pray. Thank you, God, for seeing what love and peace can do in our lives and in the entire world. We know that you want everyone to be able to have love and peace in their lives. Help us to let your love and peace grow in us each day, so that we may share with others. Amen.

TOSSED TOGETHER BY GOD

Scripture:	Romans 12:1-13
Lectionary Day:	Proper 17, Sunday between August 28 and September 3 inclusive, Year A
Topic:	God's Family; God's Gifts; Sharing Talents
Illustration:	Salad bowl (especially with garden-style salad inside)

Overview:

The variety of God's gifts for God's people is the theme of today's meditation, as rooted in the description of the body of Christ by the apostle Paul in the letter to the Romans.

The illustration is a garden salad in a bowl. Its purpose is to show how the many different ingredients all mixed together in the one bowl make a healthy food. Likewise, God's family is comprised of many different people with a variety of talents, and when everyone works together in the unity of Christ, then God's family is healthy.

Both diversity and unity are implicit in the apostle Paul's image of the church as the body of Christ. Both should be emphasized, though there may be a need on occasion to stress one more than the other. This lesson seeks to underscore both, but if there is a sense that one needs greater attention—be it the unity of the Body or the variety of gifts—then that emphasis can be given in the course of the lesson.

Narrative:

Do you like salad? (*Be prepared for some children to answer yes and others to indicate no.*) Good, I'm glad that some of you do. Salad is a really healthy food, isn't it?

Salads are really pretty mixed up, aren't they? But that's what makes them so good. All the different ingredients working together make a great salad. And one that's tasty and healthy. What do you see in this salad? (*Allow a few moments for the children to identify the various ingredients.*) All those things together make for a healthy salad.

Well, when God's people are all tossed together, it's really healthy too. Just like a good tossed salad. Our Bible lesson today reminds us that there are many different kinds of people in God's family. And God has given each one of them different gifts. That means that God has given each of us special gifts too. Isn't that exciting?

We see many people sharing their gifts each Sunday, don't we? (*At this point, you may wish to ask the children to list some of the gifts they see—that is, what they see people doing to serve. An alternative is simply to offer a listing yourself*). People share their gifts in many ways.

Some people sing. Some greet others. Some read Scripture. Some play musical instruments. Some distribute worship bulletins. Some help to decorate our worship place. Some teach Sunday school. Some prepare refreshments. Some collect the offering. Some serve Communion.

And many people share their gifts in other ways throughout the week. Some people visit those who are sick. Some lead Bible studies. Some deliver meals to people who need food. Some help others find a house to live in. Some give money to help people buy things they need to live. Some spend time helping people in many other ways. There are so many different ways God gives us to help others.

You see, when God gives us a gift, God also gives us an opportunity to use that gift to help someone else. So, this week, let's all think about the special talents God has given us, and how we can help serve other people by sharing our talents.

Prayer:

Let's pray. Dear God, we thank you that you have created all of us here today. And we are glad that you have given special gifts to all of us. Help us this week to use the special talents you give us to help others, so that many others may know of your great love. Amen.

SPECIAL GEAR AND GIFTS (OR, PROTECTIVE CLOTHING)

Scripture:	Ephesians 6:10-20
Lectionary Day:	Proper 17, Sunday between August 28 and September 3 inclusive, Year B
Topic:	Christian Character; God's Protection; Mission; Prayer
Illustration:	Baseball catcher's gear

Overview:

Today's lesson revolves around one of the most symbolic and cosmic exhortations we encounter in the Bible. No doubt, a discussion of the presence of spiritual and political "powers and principalities" is beyond the purview of children, and thus cannot be the focus of the meditation at hand. Yet the emphasis on those aspects of discipleship that are identified as keeping us in the strength of God is indeed pertinent and understandable.

The message to be highlighted, then, centers on being strong in God. The focus is on lifting up the importance of a "protective covering," as it were, of truth, righteousness, peace, faith, salvation, and prayer. These elements constitute special clothing, spiritually speaking, for Christians. In one sense, these elements are qualities of discipleship, but in another sense, they are gifts from God that provide strength for us in our journey in the world.

The illustration of baseball catcher's gear seems an appropriate way to communicate the need to be well prepared for the challenges before us. In baseball, the catcher is able to perform the functions of that position on the team only through the use of the protective clothing. The catcher's gear is a given. So are God's gifts of strength for the Christian.

Similarly, as disciples of Christ, we become and remain prepared in God's strength through our attention to truth, righteousness, peace, faith, salvation, and prayer. These elements in our experience constitute a kind of protective preparation that allows us to walk in the strength of God.

Children can understand that a baseball catcher needs special equipment. The intent is to underscore that Christians need special strength from God, and that this strength resides in the protective elements, outlined in the Epistle to the Ephesians, that God provides as gifts to us.

Narrative:

Do some of you play baseball? (*Acknowledge nods and any shows of hands.*) How many positions are there on a baseball field? (*Give the children a brief moment to answer. They may quickly answer nine, or ten if they count the batter.*) Which player wears this kind of an outfit? (*Show catcher's gear, especially mask, chest protector, and shin guards.*) That's right, the catcher. Why do you suppose a catcher has to wear all this? (*Let the children have a brief moment to respond, then proceed.*) Exactly, all this gear protects the catcher. The gear provides protection so that the catcher can catch and throw the ball without being afraid of getting hurt. Catcher's gear is very important for protecting us when we play baseball.

In today's Bible reading, the Bible talks about something like catcher's gear. The Bible talks about special clothing called armor, which is meant to protect people. What the Bible means is that we can be protected by God. We have special protection from God. This is our gear as Christians.

Just as the catcher has gear for protection, so do we as members of God's family. The gear that the Bible talks about isn't real clothing, is it? No, this biblical gear is God's strength that God gives us. So, special gifts from God provide us with the gear we need to live our lives.

What are some of these gifts? Well, the Bible lesson today talks about some really important ones: truth, righteousness, peace, faith, salvation, and prayer. Wow, that's a lot of important things for us, isn't it! All these things together keep us strong in God.

We can have God's strength to help us in our lives through all these things that God gives. Truth is what God says. Righteousness means knowing how to do what's right. Peace means getting along with other people. Faith means trusting God. Salvation is experiencing God's love. And prayer means talking with God. These are great gifts, aren't they? By giving us all these things, God gives us strength for each day.

So, when we gather each Sunday, we should think about how we can receive all these good gifts from God, so that we can make them a part of our lives and be strong in God.

Prayer:

Let's pray. Dear God, we are so glad that you have given us so many wonderful gifts to help us live each day. Thanks for helping us to be strong. Fill us with your goodness every day, so that we can grow in your love and strength. Amen.

"God wants us to learn about peace
and to practice peace. "

ORDINARY TIME AND AUTUMN

GATHERING IN THE NAME OF JESUS

Scripture:	Matthew 18:20
Lectionary Day:	Proper 18, Year A
Topic:	Church; Church Symbols; Jesus' Name; Jesus' Presence; Worship
Illustration:	The "IHS" insignia as represented on one or more of the following: the pulpit, the Communion table or tablecloth, a banner, a liturgical stole, or some other article in the worship setting

Overview:

The purpose of this lesson is to help explain one of the common symbols in the Christian worship setting and to show how it reminds us of the presence of Jesus with us.

We begin by looking at the IHS insignia as represented in the worship setting. The children can be given a brief opportunity to identify what it means, and then you can explain it. Since many of the adults also do not know its origin and meaning, this will interest them as well. Once the insignia has been identified as bespeaking the (first three letters—iota, eta, sigma—of the) name of Jesus, it can then be linked as symbol to the promise of Jesus to be present wherever two or three are gathered in Jesus' name. This connection helps underscore one of the central purposes of Christian worship: to gather in the name of Jesus with brothers and sisters of faith and experience God's love together.

Narrative:

Good morning, everyone. Today I want to talk to you about something you might see every Sunday but not pay much attention to. (*Point out IHS insignia.*) Have some of you seen this before? Do you know what it means? It looks like three letters, doesn't it? Well, you're right, it is. But you know what, they aren't English letters. How many of you have heard of the Greek language? Well now, you might have heard people who don't understand something say, "It's all Greek to me." That means they're confused.

But we don't have to be confused. These letters are rather simple but very important. You see, part of the Bible was originally written in the Greek language. These three letters are the first three letters (iota, eta, and sigma) of the name of Jesus. They're kind of like initials. We all have initials for our name, don't we? (*Some of the children may volunteer their initials; acknowledge them and then continue.*) Initials represent our whole name. These three letters are like initials and represent the name of Jesus.

For many years, churches throughout the world have used these letters to represent the name of Jesus. That way, no matter what country people are in, or what language they use, the name of Jesus can be recognized by everyone in the church family.

You see, God's family stretches all over the world and isn't limited to any one place, nation, or language. These special letters from the Bible remind us that Jesus is with all of God's people everywhere.

It's good to be able to see these letters to remind us of the name of Jesus. That way, we may be reminded of what Jesus promised in today's Bible lesson. Jesus said, "Where two or three are gathered in my name, I am there with them." That's a great promise. That means that every time we gather in the name of Jesus to worship God, we can be sure that Jesus is with us.

So, remember that every Sunday when we get together. When you see the IHS letters, you can remember that Jesus has promised to be with us. And when Jesus is with us, we can expect some good things to happen.

Prayer:

Let's pray. Dear God, we are glad that Jesus has promised to be with us whenever we gather together in Jesus' name. Thank you that we can join together in your family and enjoy your love. Be with us this week and help us to show your love to others. Amen.

A LIGHT FOR FINDING OUR WAY

Scripture:	Psalm 119:105
Lectionary Day:	Proper 18, Sunday between September 4 and 10 inclusive, Year B
Topic:	Bible; God's Light; God's Word
Illustration:	Flashlight

Overview:

Today's illustration is an obvious and well-known one: a flashlight. Children very likely have recently made use of a flashlight during a camping trip or week at summer camp. To talk about the function of a flashlight should be quite natural. Allowing the children some time to share their summer experiences may also be a good bonding exercise (for the whole congregation—especially as some of the children may share about summer camp, and the church, which hopefully supports the children through a camp fund, needs to hear and celebrate the positive experiences of camp).

To liken a flashlight to God's word is the key to this meditation. The lesson centers around an important function of both: to show us the way. In the case of a flashlight, its function is to show us the way at night while we are out in the dark. In the case of God's word, especially as the Bible, the purpose is to show us the way to walk through life.

The pathway in this respect is God's will, and the Bible as a light is what illumines, reveals, and shows forth the way to go—that is, live. In this, the Bible not only shows us God's will, but also shows us God. For in showing us the way along life's path, the Bible also shows us God and how we may relate to God.

Narrative:

Good morning. The sun sure is shining brightly today, isn't it? (Or *if it's a cloudy day, maybe say something like "Where's all the sunshine today?"*) Look what I've brought with me this morning. (*Show flashlight.*) What is it? (*Pause for a response.*) Do you suppose I'll need this flashlight this morning? No, probably not. It's pretty bright here, isn't it?

What do you use a flashlight for? (*Let the children make a few suggestions.*) Did some of you use a flashlight this summer? (*Let some of the children tell briefly of their experiences camping or at summer camp.*) It's really important to have a flashlight to see at night when we're in the woods or at the beach and trying to find our way back to our campsite or cabin.

Usually, we have a path to follow. But we need to be able to see the path, don't we? That's why it's best to shine the flashlight on the ground right in front of us, isn't it? Sometimes you see someone shining a flashlight up at the sky. But that doesn't help them see where they're going, does it? No, you need to keep your flashlight shining on the pathway ahead of you, so that you can see where you're going, and so that you can get where you're going safely.

Well, you know, the Bible is a lot like a flashlight. For the Bible tells us about God and God's word. In today's Bible lesson, we're told that God's word is like a light that shines to light up the path before us. That means God's word, which we can read in the Bible, points the way for us to live. It shows us how to follow God and how to do what God thinks is best.

That's why the Bible is so important to us, and why we read it carefully every week. It helps us see which way to go in our lives. It helps us see what God wants us to do. And so it helps us learn about God and about life.

That's how the Bible is just like a flashlight. So, next time you're using a flashlight, remember your Bible. And next time your reading your Bible, remember that it can help us see what God wants us to see and what God wants us to do.

Prayer:

Let's pray. Dear God, thank you for sunlight that lights our days. And thank you for giving us your Word, which gives us light to see what's important in life. Help us to read our Bible and to see in it your light for our lives. Amen.

LOVE FINDING WHAT'S LOST

Scripture:	Luke 15:1-10
Lectionary Day:	Proper 19, Sunday between September 11 and 17 inclusive, Year C
Topic:	Equality; Forgiveness; God's Love; Seeking God; Sin
Illustration:	Ten coins (or other small objects)

Overview:

The three "lost and found" parables of Luke 15 are among the most cherished of the stories told by Jesus. In each parable, there are those who are lost and need to be found. There is a lost sheep, a lost coin, and lost sons (the younger, wasteful son and the older, spiteful son, both of whom are "lost" to their father).

In each parable, there is also a poignant picture of God and God's love. There is God as a responsible shepherd, God as a diligent woman, and God as a forgiving father. At the core of each story is the seeking love of God.

That seeking love of God is highlighted in today's meditation for children. Making use of ten coins (or other similar objects), the lesson endeavors to emphasize God's impartial and imploring love for everyone. In other words, God's love seeks us out when we're lost. And God's love finds us and restores us. The restoration of relationship is at the heart of God's love.

Prior to the children's lesson time, be sure to hide one of the coins (or other objects) in an place easy for the children to locate. After showing them the nine left, ask them to help you locate the one that's missing. Then you can discuss with them why finding the lost one is important, so that all ten can be together.

This conversation then leads to a discussion of God's seeking love. The intent is to help the children understand that God really loves us and will seek us out when we've gone astray. God's love means forgiveness. This means that we can approach God and need not try to hide from God. God loves us all equally and wants us all to be part of God's family. That surely is something to celebrate. Just like the woman in the story rejoiced.

Narrative:

Hello. How is everyone today? (*Pause briefly for responses.*) Good. I'm fine, too. But there is one thing not so fine. See what I've got here. (*Show them the nine coins.*) Can you count how many I have? (*Let the children count together.*) Right, there's nine here. But I had ten. I'm missing one. And I need all ten to be together. Could you help me find the missing one? I know it must be around here someplace. (*Pause for a brief search; if one of the children does not find the coin quickly, then stumble upon it yourself and continue.*)

Hey, we found it! Thanks for all your help. Now we have all ten coins together. Sometimes we may think we have enough, so if we lose something, like a small coin, we won't miss it. But, you know, God loves us all equally. And God doesn't want to lose any of us. We are all important to God. Jesus told a story about that.

Once there was a woman who had ten coins. Every coin was important to her. When she lost one, she cleaned her whole house looking for it. When she found it, she was glad. She called her friends and neighbors together and they all rejoiced. She said, "Rejoice with me, for I have found the coin that I had lost." And Jesus concluded the story by saying, "Just so, I tell you, there is joy in the presence of the angels of God over one sinner who repents."

Isn't that a great story? It reminds us that God really loves us. God is like the woman in the story who searched for her missing coin. God's love seeks out each one of us.

Sometimes we get a little lost. We sort of lose our way. We make mistakes. We feel confused and think we're lost. But God can find us. God wants us to know that we can always find our way back to God. That's because God loves us and will forgive us. God loves us all the same. God's love seeks us out and rejoices when we come home to God.

Now, that's something to celebrate, isn't it? Let's thank God for such seeking love.

Prayer:

Let's pray. Dear God, we are so glad that you love all of us. Thank you that you love us all equally, and that each of us is important to you. Help us whenever we make mistakes or feel confused to look for your love, for we know that your love will find us. Amen.

GOD IS MY NIGHTLIGHT

Scripture:	Psalm 27:1-6
Lectionary Day:	Proper 20, Sunday between September 18 and 24 inclusive, Year B; (also Third Sunday after Epiphany, Year A)
Topic:	God's Light; Trusting God
Illustration:	A nightlight (especially the kind that turns on automatically in response to darkness)

Overview:

Psalm 27's affirmation that "Yahweh [God's personal covenant name] is my light and my salvation" is among the best-known and comforting statements of Scripture. The psalm is an assertive song of confidence in God. It is this confidence in God that the children's message seeks to highlight.

The illustrative object is a nightlight. Many children are familiar with nightlights. They understand the sense of comfort and confidence they bring to a bedroom at night, even if they have never really stopped to think about it. This lesson gives them a brief opportunity to think about it in relationship to an analogy with God as a "nightlight" in whom we may place our confidence and take comfort.

The lesson begins with an identification of the object and a brief conversation concerning its use. Then the psalm's affirmation about God being our light is cited. The discussion follows from that point, with the intention of highlighting God's reliability as a sure source of confidence and comfort. Indeed, God is our light for life.

Narrative:

What's this? (*Show the nightlight.*) Right, a nightlight. Do some of you have nightlights at your house? I do. I even have some lights outside that automatically come on when it gets dark. And this nightlight does the same thing inside. (*Show nightlight again.*) As soon as the room gets dark, the light comes on. (*If it's possible to plug in the nightlight and then darken the room, you may be able to show the children how it works automatically. This, of course, is an optional exercise.*) That's a great nightlight, don't you agree?

What's a nightlight good for? (*Pause for a few responses.*) Good. I think a nightlight is great because it gives off just enough light in the dark so we can see a little. That way we don't have to be afraid of the dark. We can feel confident and comfortable, right?

Well, you know, God is like a nightlight. That's sort of how God is described in today's Bible lesson. God is our light, says the Bible. God is a light who automatically is there with us whenever it gets dark. And so the Bible tells us that with God as our light, we don't need to be afraid. We can be confident and comfortable. Don't you think that's great? We can trust God to be our light and strength each day.

Prayer:

Let's pray. Thank you, God, for being our light. We are glad that you are always shining in our lives. Help us to see better by your light how we should live each day. And help us to be good friends to others, so that they can see your light and be part of your family. Amen.

GOD'S SURPRISE

Scripture:	Matthew 19:30 or Mark 9:35
Lectionary Day:	Proper 20, Sunday between September 18 and 24 inclusive, Year B
Topic:	Caring for Others; Discipleship; Priorities; Trusting God
Illustration:	The activity of making a line and distributing candy or fruit

Overview:

This lesson, like the Bible verse in today's reading, has a bit of a surprise twist to it. It entails having the children make a line in response to your invitation to line up for some candy or fruit. The twist comes when you begin the distribution at the end of the line. This will serve to dramatize and introduce the biblical passage for further discussion.

The reading from the Gospel is brief but poignant. Its focus is the meaning of greatness. It asserts that greatness resides in servanthood and childhood. This, of course, was a startling assertion by Jesus in its original setting, and it is no less so today. It strikes at the heart of what human culture tends to value. Human society, ancient and modern, lifts up might, power, wealth, and prestige as premier values and aspirations. These are seen as the source of greatness in a world where people compete to be recognized and rewarded.

Yet Jesus lifts up the more lowly realities of being a servant and a child, and designates these as great. The qualities of servant and child make one great, according to Jesus. This is a complete twist and reversal of common human values and expectations. It is this twist that the children's lesson seeks to underscore through the dramatic exercise and subsequent conversation.

In addition to the primary focus of the meditation, this lesson has the added benefit of emphasizing the value of children. This is an important affirmation in the biblical text, and one that serves as a reminder, not only to the children but also to the whole congregation, of the importance of treating, welcoming, and supporting children as significant members of God's family. This Bible lesson, then, provides part of an ongoing reminder of the important presence and example that children provide for the people of God. This affirmation can help nurture an ongoing commitment to children in the life of the local church.

Narrative:

I've got a surprise for you today. Let's line up here. (*Quickly point out a spot.*) I've got some fruit (or candy) to give out. Aha, here's a surprise! The line starts here. (*Go to the end of the line and point it out as the beginning.*) Did I surprise you a bit? (*Distribute the fruit or candy to each child and continue with the discussion.*)

A surprise is just what happened in our Bible lesson today. Jesus surprised everyone by saying, "The first shall be last, and the last shall be first." Well, now, what does that mean? For one thing, it means that God can surprise us. God doesn't play by our rules all the time. God can do something different to surprise us.

What's more, God wants us to surprise one another. God encourages us not to try always to be first. Instead, God wants us to look out for other people. You know, help others first. Don't push and shove our way to the front of the line. Be respectful of others. Share.

We live in a world where people think that being powerful, or wealthy, or strong makes them great. And people often compete with other people to try to be better than others. But Jesus surprises us all by saying that the best way to be great is to be like a child who trusts God. To be great is to be like a servant who helps others. That's a whole different way of thinking, isn't it? God gives us a whole new definition of greatness, and invites us to be great in love, faith, and service.

You see, God loves all of us and wants us to get along with each other. When we look out for others, we can be sure that God looks out for us. Sometimes it may seem that by helping others we end up last in line. So what! We know that God will take care of us. And this means that we will really be first, because God is our first priority. And when we concentrate on trusting God and helping others, we never know what God might do. God may surprise us with something better!

Prayer:

Let's pray. Dear God, thank you for surprising us. Help us to learn the best way to live. Help us to trust you and not worry about ourselves. Help us to help others. Amen.

Doing What We Say

Scripture:	Matthew 21:28-32
Lectionary Day:	Proper 21, Sunday between September 25 and October 1 inclusive, Year A
Topic:	Faith; God's Will; Obedience
Illustration:	A wastebasket, dish towel, or other household chore related item

Overview:

Today's lesson revolves around the parable of the two sons told by Jesus soon after the triumphal entry into Jerusalem and the cleansing of the temple. The parable is part of a collection of stories in Matthew's Gospel that highlight the distinction between the profession and practice of faith.

Begin the lesson by sharing the objects you have brought. One or two is sufficient to get the children talking briefly about household chores. Some may have regular chores assigned to them, and some may not, but all understand something about chores being done around the house. This point of illustration, then, sets the stage for the biblical story itself.

Tell the story offered by Jesus in the parable of the two sons. Translate the story to contemporary circumstances, for instance, by substituting work or chores that the children would understand. The point, of course, is not the specific chores per se. At issue is obedience, the proper response to God's will. Through the story, then, this question is raised: "How do we do what God wants?"

The strong rebuttal implied in the story is that it is not sufficient simply to profess faith in God. One must act on that faith and respond to God's will. This is the same theme stated emphatically by Jesus in Matthew 7:21-29 and later reiterated by James in 1:22-27 of his epistle. It is this emphasis on an active faith responsive to God's will that is at the heart of the message being shared in a simple but direct manner with the children.

Narrative:

Good morning. What do you think I have this morning? (*Show the item or items you have brought that represent household chores.*) What do you suppose these things are for? (*Give the children a moment to make suggestions.*) Very good. These are things we use in doing chores around our house. Do some of you do household chores? Good, I'm glad to know that many of us are pitching in to help with work in our homes. It helps a lot when families can cooperate together to get the household chores done.

You know, Jesus told a lot of stories about families. In today's Bible lesson, Jesus tells a story about two children. A father went to one of his sons and said, "I need you to do some work for me today." The son said, "I will not." But later he changed his mind and did the work. The father went to his other son and said, "I need you to do some work for me today." This other son answered, "I will do it." But then he never did any of the work.

Jesus ended the story with a question: "Which of the two sons did the will of his father?" What do you think? (*Children may have different answers, but be prepared and prompt in affirming the correct one.*) That's right, the first son who actually did the work.

Jesus was trying to teach us that it's important to practice our faith in God and not just talk about it. How do we do what God wants? That's right, by doing what God says. It's important to say what we believe, but it's even more important to do what we say we believe.

Wouldn't it have been good if both sons had said they would do the work for their father, and then both did it? Sure, that would be great. So, let's remember that it's important to try to do God's will. And it's important to do what we say and do our share of the chores, too.

Prayer:

Let's pray. Dear God, thank you for the stories Jesus told. We don't always like doing chores, but we are glad to learn about you and your love. Help us to do what you tell us is right, so that we may share your love with other people. Amen.

GOD'S BANQUET OF LOVE

Scripture: Matthew 22:1-10; Luke 14:1-24

Lectionary Day: Proper 23, Sunday between October 9
and 15 inclusive, Year A; Proper 17,
Sunday between August 28 and Septem-
ber 3 inclusive, Year C

Topic: Equality; God's Love; Mission; Worship

Illustration: Banquet, wedding, or party invitation (or
other items—such as party favors, bal-
loons, streamers, decorated paper
plates—that represent a party)

Overview:

Today's meditation is prompted by the banquet parables of
the Gospels of Matthew and Luke. These stories told by Jesus
have a biting edge that draws a demarcation between those
entering the kingdom of heaven and those not. This is especially true in Matthew's account. Consequently, the message
of the entire parable is too much for children.

The analogy between God's kingdom and a great banquet,
however, is one that is a helpful picture for children in understanding that God invites people to a great purpose. So while
the judgment part of the parables is too harsh and confusing
for children, the inviting part is compelling and appropriate.

Begin the lesson with the items you have brought to represent a party of some sort. Discuss with the children some
of the features of a party gathering. Try to encourage them to
think in terms of the blessing that a group of people can
share when gathered together in gratitude and graciousness
toward one another.

Move from the illustration to the theme of God's kingdom as a banquet of love. Emphasize that God invites many
people and wants everyone to respond and join in the celebration of love. But some choose not to participate, and so
they miss out. We, however, want to respond to God's invitation to come and join in the celebration of love.

In a sense, every Sunday when we gather in worship, we
dedicate ourselves anew to the celebration of love and the
work of God's kingdom. Underscoring that God's love is the

continual basis for our worship and work, attitudes and actions may reinforce this idea. In responding to God's invitation, celebration and commitment go hand in hand.

Narrative:

Have you ever been to a party? (*Give the children a moment to respond, then quickly show them the party-related things you have brought.*) Here are some things you might see at a party. What are they? (*Let the children briefly identify a few things.*) Parties are great fun, aren't they? Whether it's a wedding, a birthday party, or some kind of gathering of friends and family, it's great to get people together to celebrate and have fun.

Did you know that the Bible talks about a party when describing our relationship with God? Jesus told a number of stories where God's kingdom is described as a great banquet or party. It's like God is inviting people to come together to celebrate God's love. Doesn't that sound like a great party? (*Pause only for quick nods from the children.*)

God says, "Come, enjoy the love I offer. And learn to share that love with others. Come, be my guests in the banquet of love. And then go be my servants in sharing the feast of love with others." God invites us to a great purpose. God invites us to love.

When God hosts a party, God invites everyone. No one is excluded by God. The only way to miss out is not to show up. God says, "Come and celebrate." Anyone who says no misses out.

But we don't want to miss out, do we? And we don't want others to miss out; that's why we invite others and welcome everyone who wants to gather with us in celebrating God's love. We want to enjoy God's love forever.

Every Sunday when we gather for worship, we celebrate God's love. And we learn more about God's love, so that we can better share that love with others throughout the week.

Prayer:

Let's pray. Dear God, thank you so much for inviting us to your banquet of love. We are glad to be able to celebrate your love. Help us to invite others and welcome everyone who wishes to join with us in learning about your love. Amen.

SEEKING THE BEST

Scripture:	Philippians 4:1-9
Lectionary Day:	Proper 23, Sunday between October 9 and 15 inclusive, Year A
Topic:	Christian Character; God's Will; Potential; Priorities
Illustration:	A blue ribbon, trophy or some other kind of special first-prize item

Overview:

In the letters of the apostle Paul we find a number of metaphors for faith associated with running a race. In the letter to the Philippians a similar image is shared when Paul asserts, "I press on toward the goal for the prize of the heavenly call of God in Christ Jesus" (3:14). The picture of faith and salvation as constituting a journey, a challenge, a quest is presented in different ways throughout the New Testament Scriptures.

Today's children's meditation picks up on this image and engages it in terms of Paul's words about seeking what's best, discerning what's excellent—a theme that fills the letter to the Philippians (1:10; 4:8). The intent is to help the children reflect on the many excellent qualities of character and conduct that Paul cites in Philippians 4:8-9.

Begin the lesson with a quick identification of the illustrative objects and a discussion of their association with a variety of contests. Then move to a conversation about seeking what's excellent by doing our best. The point is not to emphasize winning or competition, but to encourage a discerning of what's good, right, excellent, and worthy of our best efforts. These, of course, are precisely what Paul emphasizes.

Narrative:

Anyone recognize this? Yes, it's a blue ribbon (trophy, prize, etc.). It's something you might get when you've done really well in a contest. Maybe a spelling contest at school. Or a sports event. Or a special project, or a writing contest, or a cake baking contest. Have some of you been in activities that have prizes like this? (*Give the children a few moments to mention their experiences.*) Prizes like this are often given to people who do really well and maybe come in first in an event. There could be all kinds of things to be involved in, right?

Well, in today's Bible reading we hear about things that are first. But it's not talking about coming in first in a race or in anything. The point isn't about knowing how to win a contest. It's about knowing how to choose what's best. Knowing what's most important. To put important things first in our lives.

What do you think are some of the important things the Bible tells us about? (*Let the children have a few moments to list some possibilities; encourage and affirm them in their answers such as "love one another, be kind, be fair," etc.*) Well, there are really lots of good things that the Bible tells us are important.

In today's Bible reading, we have a brief list of some things that are really important. We're told to concentrate on whatever is true, honorable, pure, pleasing, commendable, excellent, and praiseworthy. Wow, that's quite a list, isn't it!

These are a lot of good things to put first in our lives, don't you agree? They tell us what's most important to God. What's best for us to think about and do. Just imagine if we were always trying to think of what's best. And we were trying to do what's best. Do you think that we could do that this week? I bet that we can, with God's help. Then we can really do our best.

Prayer:

Let's pray. O God, you're the best. You always do what's right and excellent. Help us to learn more of what to put first. And help us to do our best to do what's right. Amen.

IN TRAINING (OR, GOD'S GYM)

Scripture:	2 Timothy 3:14-17
Lectionary Day:	Proper 24, Sunday between October 16 and 22 inclusive, Year C
Topic:	Bible; God's Word; Spiritual Growth
Illustration:	Some kind of training equipment, such as ankle weights or a small exercise tool, along with a bound Bible (with strings or elastics to keep the Bible closed)

Overview:

Today's meditation focuses on the importance of the Bible as a regular reference point in our spiritual growth. The text from 2 Timothy 3:16-17 offers a clear statement of the role of Scripture for "training in righteousness" toward the goal of being "equipped for every good work." The intention of this children's lesson is to present and emphasize these points.

The lesson begins with a twofold discussion centered on the illustrations. First, share the item of exercise equipment that you have brought. Briefly note something of the benefits of exercise in training and in preparing yourself to be healthy and to do well in certain activities. Then move the discussion toward a view of the Bible as a training manual designed to help us be prepared to follow God and do God's will.

This part of the discussion can then include the second illustration. Show the bound Bible and ask if it could be very helpful in this condition. The point is to underscore that for the Bible to be of any value, we must read and study it regularly. We must open the Bible and then open ourselves to what God would teach us. Then we can really be trained to do what's right and do good things for others, as God wants us to.

It might be that this lesson would serve as a corollary to giving to some of the children a Bible or Scripture portion, or some other kind of scripturally based devotional, as appropriate. Of course, it may be that such presentations may occur on another occasion. If so, it might be a helpful reinforcement to have 2 Timothy 3:16-17 printed in large print on a full page of paper for distribution to the children (and their families) as a reminder of the lesson.

Narrative:

This morning I've got a couple things to show you. Who knows what this is? (*Show one of the items of exercise equipment.*) That's right, it's a ———. Do you know what you use it for? (*Pause briefly for children to make suggestions, and then offer an explanation.*) Exercise equipment can be helpful in keeping us in good health, can't it? (*Show another item of exercise equipment at this time, if you have more than one to share.*)

Do you think it's important to exercise? (*Let children briefly respond, then continue.*) Exercise helps us stay healthy. But do you know what? It can also help us prepare our bodies to do things—like run faster, play catch with a ball, or play other sports games. Exercise is a kind of training. It helps our bodies get healthier and stronger.

But did you know that there is also training for our minds? Yes. You train your mind every day when you go to school, don't you? Training both our bodies and our minds is important to growing up and being able to do all sorts of things in our lives.

In our Bible lesson today, there is something mentioned that is very important for God's people to use in their training to be Christians. Do you know what it is? That's right, the Bible. The Bible is like a training manual for God's people. It helps us learn what's good, and right, and just, and kind, so that we know how best to live.

Here's a Bible. But what's wrong? (*Show the Bible that is bound with strings or elastics.*) Would this Bible be very helpful for our training with God? (*Some children will likely respond no.*) Why not? Right, it's all tied up. We can't open it. Now, if we don't open the Bible, it can't help us much, can it? We need to open our Bibles if we're going to use the Bible for our training, don't we? Of course we do.

The Bible is God's training manual for us. We need to open the Bible in order to read, understand, and follow it. And just as we open the Bible, so we can open ourselves to new ways of thinking and understanding. As we study the Bible, we become open to God's will and God's work in our lives. That's the most important kind of training in the whole world, isn't it?

Prayer:

Let's pray. Dear God, thank you for giving us the Bible. Help us to read and study it regularly, so that we can be well trained as your children. Amen.

BEING HONEST

Scripture:	Luke 18:9-14
Lectionary Day:	Proper 25, Sunday between October 23 and 29 inclusive, Year C
Topic:	Honesty; Humility; Worship
Illustration:	A Halloween-type mask

Overview:

This meditation centers on the parable of the Pharisee and publican. The focal point of the lesson is verse 14b: "All who exalt themselves will be humbled, but all who humble themselves will be exalted."

The lesson begins with use of a Halloween-type mask. This is to lead into a discussion about pretending to be someone else and about truly being ourselves. The brief use of this illustration then sets the stage for retelling the parable as recorded in Luke 18:9-14. Since the historical context and terms may be lost on children, it is perhaps best to relate the story in more familiar and contemporary terms.

Tell the story of the two worshipers in simple contemporary language. Underscore that God wants us to be humble and honest. God already knows who we are and what we are really like. One of the points of worship is to better understand ourselves in terms of God's understanding. So, we shouldn't compare ourselves to others. We should concern ourselves with God. That is the appropriate focus of worship.

Narrative:

(*Put mask on.*) Does anyone know who I am? (*Children should certainly indicate so.*) Did the mask fool you? No? You still knew who I was, didn't you? It's fun to use masks and costumes sometimes, isn't it? (*Allow for a brief discussion of costumes by children.*) To pretend to be someone else can be fun. But it doesn't change who we really are, does it? No, we're still the same people we really are.

And that's who we should be. God wants us to be ourselves when we come to worship, pray, and learn each Sunday. There's no sense trying to pretend we're somebody else, or trying to make ourselves out to be better than someone else. God knows who we are. A mask doesn't change who we are. It just covers up our smile. I bet that God likes our smile. Don't you think so?

In today's Bible lesson, Jesus tells a story about two people who came to worship God. The story goes like this: Two people came to worship and pray. One was a very religious person who came to worship every Sunday. One was a person with a bad reputation who seldom came to worship. The very religious person stood by himself and said, "God, I thank you that I am better than other people." But the other person stood far off in a corner and looked down and said, "Dear God, please have mercy on me, for I haven't done what's right."

Which one do you think had the right attitude for worshiping God? (*Let the children respond, then proceed.*) I agree. I think the one with the right attitude was the one who was humble and honest before God. The first person wasn't being honest. But God wants us to be humble and honest.

On Sundays, when we come to worship God, we don't come to try to impress God or make God think that we're perfect. God already knows who we are, right? Yes, and God loves us. So, we don't have to pretend to be something we're not. God invites us to be humble and honest. That way, we open ourselves to receive God's love. And isn't that the best part of worship? Yes. And you know what? We can be humble and honest with God in our prayers every day. And then we can enjoy God's love every day. Now that's something to smile about!

Prayer:

Let's pray. Dear God, thank you for creating us and inviting us to worship you. We're glad that we don't have to pretend to be perfect, because you love us and want the best for us always. Help us to be humble and honest with you and everyone. Amen.

LIFE'S ANCHOR

Scripture:	Hebrews 6:19
Lectionary Day:	*in conjunction with* Proper 25, Sunday between October 23 and 29 inclusive, Year B
Topic:	Faith; Hope; Trusting God
Illustration:	A boat anchor (or a picture of one)

Overview:

This meditation focuses on the picture of hope as an anchor. This picture is part of a somewhat lengthy and complex discussion in the Epistle to the Hebrews about the high priesthood of Jesus and the promises of God. That discussion, of course, is well beyond the scope of a children's lesson. Yet, the metaphor of an anchor as hope is one that may well serve to help children understand the nature of hope, especially in relationship to their faith and God's promises. It also poses a risk to a children's lesson to focus on the conceptual rather than the concrete. Thus, in this sense, the concept of hope must give way to the concrete practice of it.

The Scripture passage calls hope "a sure and steadfast anchor of the soul." This is a profound picture. Not all that's packed into that picture can be shared with the children in one brief setting. It's been said that to realize the worth of an anchor, you have to feel the stress of the storm. Often we associate hope with that faith which sustains us during a time of challenge or crisis. This, of course, is an important feature of hope, and one that could be explored with the use of the anchor metaphor.

This focus, however, it is not featured in this lesson. Herein, the focus is more on understanding hope as a source of stability in our lives. In this sense, the anchor represents that which is stable and steadfast in securing us. It addresses those worries and fears that many of us, including children, have from time to time. Hope in this sense is an expression of faith that secures us to God. Hope, then, anchors us in God's love. This is the point to communicate.

Begin the lesson with a conversation about the use of anchors. A listing of the characteristics and functions of an anchor may aid in this discussion. Move from this to a highlighting of the reference in Hebrews that likens hope to an anchor. A listing of the characteristics of hope may then be created by the conversation. Conclude with an affirmation of hope as the kind of faith that anchors us in God's love.

Narrative:

Who can tell me what this is? (*Show anchor, or picture of it.*) What does an anchor do? What do you use if for? (*Pause to allow for children's responses.*) Very good. An anchor is a way to tie up your boat when you're out in the water away from shore. An anchor digs into the ocean bottom and holds your boat. That way your boat can't drift away. People who go out in a boat fishing often throw out an anchor to hold their boat while they fish, right?

Well, did you know that the Bible says that hope is like an anchor? That's an interesting picture, isn't it? What's hope? (*Pause only briefly for responses; most children will not know how to put an answer into words, so be prepared to proceed quickly.*) Hope is a very special trust in God. Hope keeps us thinking about God, and thinking about God's love.

Hope links us to God. That's how hope is like an anchor. Hope is like an anchor because it keeps us secure in God's love. It means that we can trust God, no matter what happens in our lives. We don't have to worry about things, because hope is the faith that anchors us in God's love.

Prayer:

Let's pray. Dear God, thank you for loving us. We are glad that we can trust you to care for us. Help us each day to put our faith and hope in you. Amen.

Using God's Gifts

Scripture:	Matthew 25:14-30 or Luke 19:11-27
Lectionary Day:	Proper 28, Sunday between November 13 and 19 inclusive, Year A
Topic:	Discipleship; God's Gifts; Loving Others; Potential
Illustration:	A variety of round circles cut out of paper to look like money, with the word "love" written in bold letters on each "coin"

Overview:

Today's meditation is derived from the parable of the talents. A talent, from the Greek word *talanton,* represented a large sum of money. Over time, through association with the parable, the word "talent" came into English to signify a special gift or ability, something with which someone is endowed.

In referencing the parable of the talents, then, the focus herein is on these endowments, which God has given to us. There are many ways to look at the idea of endowments, but for the purpose of this brief lesson, the focus is on the qualities of personal character as well as the special gifts that we might associate with people. The parable stresses the responsibility associated with the endowment, but, for this lesson, we may emphasize more the privilege associated with God's gifts.

Narrative:

Today we're going to talk about special gifts that God gives to people. In today's Bible reading, we have a story that Jesus told about people who were given special talents.

Did you know that God has given everyone special talents? That's right. People have different gifts from God. All of us right here, too. We are each gifted in different ways. Some of us can sing beautifully. Some of us can write well. Some of us can solve math problems. Some of us can run fast. Some us can—well, let me ask you. What else do you think some of us can do well? (*Let the children respond with a brief list.*) Great!

God gives us different abilities and interests. And God gives these special things to us for a reason: not just for ourselves, but so we can share them with others. In worship, people do different things. Some lead in music; some read the Bible; some prepare the bulletins; some decorate the sanctuary; some greet people; some serve communion; and so forth.

God wants us to use our gifts to help others. Because God loves us, God gives us special talents. And because God wants us to love others, God wants us to use the talents to help others.

These talents are God's gifts to us. And do you know what the Bible says is the most important gift that God gives? Here's a clue. Look at these paper coins I made. They have the word on them that tells us what God's best gift is. What is it? Love. That's right! You can keep this paper coin as a reminder of what gift God has for you. Love is the gift that God wants to give everyone. And that's a gift we can share with everyone, isn't it?

Prayer:

Let's pray. Dear God, thank for giving us your love. And thank you for giving each of us special talents and abilities. Help us to use our talents to show love to others. Amen.

THINKING AND THANKING

Scripture:	Psalm 100
Lectionary Day:	Thanksgiving Day, Year C
Topic:	Creation; Thanksgiving; Worship
Illustration:	A poster/sign with the words "think" and "thank" printed boldly

Overview:

The notion of giving thanks to God is the theme of this meditation. Referencing Psalm 100 (though many other psalms and Scriptures would be equally relevant), the lesson intends to underscore the connection between thinking about God and thanking God. Both, of course, are central to the attitudes and actions of worship. In addition, the two words are closely related. Both are etymologically related to the Old English "thought." This connection is illustrated for the children with the poster/sign featuring both words.

The two illustrated words, then, become the starting point for the lesson. After inquiring with the children as to the difference between the two words (in spelling, meaning, etc.), you can underscore their close connection by telling of their origin in the word "thought" or "thoughtful."

The point of the illustration is to link "thinking" about God and "thanking" God. This can further be done through reference to Psalm 100, where worshipers are encouraged to be glad and thankful toward God. Highlighting those parts of the psalm that encourage praise and thanksgiving reinforce the emphasis on being thankful people. Some discussion of what the children think is entailed in being thankful may appropriately flow from this conversation.

As part of the discussion, it is important to point out that the psalm clearly presents to us good reasons for thinking about God and thanking God. God has created us. God makes us part of God's family. God is good. God's love is enduring, and God is faithful to us. Underscoring these themes may help the children understand the basis for regular worship and thankfulness.

Narrative:

Do any of you recognize these words? (*Show the poster/sign with the words "think" and "thank" in big, bold letters.*) What are they? That's right, they are the words "think" and "thank." Do they look alike? Yes, they do. They're almost twins, aren't they?

Did you know that the word "think" and the word "thank" really are related? They both come from an Old English word that means "thought." Both "think" and "thank" mean to be thoughtful. When we think, we have a thought about something. When we thank someone, we have a thought of appreciation toward someone. And we want to let them know that we're thinking of them, so we say "thank you." That lets them know that we are glad about them.

How do you feel when you feel thankful? What do you do? (*Let the children respond briefly.*) When we say "thank you" to someone, we are letting that person know that we are thinking about them, and are glad that they have been so nice to us. When we thank someone, how do you think that makes that person feel? Right, they feel good that we've thought about them.

Well, you know, the Bible is always telling us to thank God. Today's Bible reading is Psalm 100, which invites us to praise and thank God. Did you know that a psalm is really a special kind of song? In this psalm, we are invited to come worship and thank God with gladness and singing.

But some people misunderstand the psalm, you know. They think it says, "Worship God with grumpiness," instead of gladness. "Come into God's presence with sighing," instead of singing. But that's because they're thinking about themselves and not thinking about God.

The Bible encourages us to think about God. When we think about God, we remember that God made us, that God is good, that God's love lasts forever, and that God is faithful to care for us. That's a lot of good reasons to be thankful, don't you agree? Right, that's just what the Bible is trying to tell us: Think about God. Thank God. Worship God. Be glad. Be full of song. Know that God loves us. Praise God. And be thankful.

So, do you think we can be "thinking and thanking" people? Sure we can! Be both thoughtful and thankful as you work and play this week.

Prayer:

Let's pray. Dear God, we know that you have made each one of us, and that you want us to think about you and thank you for all your goodness. Thank you for loving us. Help us to think about your love by thanking you and others who show your love to us. Amen.

"In responding to God's invitation,
celebration and commitment go hand in hand."

MOVEMENT

UNDERTAKING THE UNFOLDING JOURNEY

The gospel of Christ is not just a message. It is a movement. In the Good News, there is a possibility of new life. The new is good; the goodness is new. The Good News is rooted in relationship to God's love and is experienced through relationship with God's people. This is the movement. The message is but a means. New life through relationship is the goal.

Christian proclamation, then, is not a destination, but rather, a pilgrimage. At the heart of the Good News is an ever-new relationship. The relationship is the reality of faith and love that we embrace in response to the forgiveness and love offered by God. This relationship is always a journey and never a stagnant pool. This is equally true in our undertakings with children through the weekly worship and meditation. The message we share does not begin or end with words. It is rooted and realized in a relationship that is ongoing and unfolding. In making and renewing this affirmation, we become prepared for undertaking the journey.

At the heart of our undertaking is the nurture of a reality and experience of faith and love expressed in relationship to God and one another. Faith and love are nurtured in the community of faith where the love of Christ reigns. This, then, is both the context and content for children's messages. Hopefully, this has been evident in our menu of meditations. In concluding, perhaps I can reiterate a few points to ponder as a means of reflection for the continuing journey.

Through the message and method we seek a movement. We endeavor to be nourished in God's love, so that we may grow in God's love. This nourishment is a kind of "solid food" (Hebrews 5:14) by which we feed together on God's grace and are strengthened in our life in the community of faith. There is a structure and substance to this nourishment that I have sought to underscore and unfold in our menu of

153

meditations, and which must ever be sought in sharing them with the children in our communities of faith. Let me close the discussion by reflecting summarily on the structure and substance of this nourishment.

---

*"We endeavor to be nourished in God's love,
so that we may grow in God's love."*

The structural aspect of the nourishment we seek constitutes a support. It is the flesh and bones of our enterprise, whereas the substance is the heart and soul. Yet in human relationships the structure greatly shapes the substance. In reflecting on the structure of children's meditations, I offer three summary points for consideration.

First, a consistent practice is an important aspect of the structure of nourishment. Just as we need to eat regularly and according to helpful and healthy routines, so our approach to children's meditations must partake of a certain consistency of practice. I have commented in various ways about the ingredients of the approach we may take. I need not repeat those points here. We need only remind ourselves that a consistent practice of preparation and sharing is important to the value of the experience. This in no way suggests redundancy or squelches variety; it simply underscores the importance of a regular practice of study and sharing as critical to the structure of children's meditations.

Second, concerted progress is our intent. There is a growing together in God's word that is at the structural center of our target with each children's meditation. In this regard, a children's message is not a disjointed entity. It is a concerted effort from week to week that is constitutive of the rhythm of worship, learning, community, mission, and growth that is indispensable to the structure of the Christian church. We are on a journey, and so need to be aware of where we've been and are going together. Lessons build on each other and are pieced together with a goal toward progress in faith and love. We must be reminded that the message is a bridge to unfolding relationships. We would do well to monitor our progress concerning what bridges we have crossed, and which still need crossing. Each message is a thread, but our overall perspective is the tapestry we seek to fashion.

Above all, then, at the structural core of our meditations is the continual pathway we tread. This bespeaks the vision that illumines our way. We see beyond where we are or have been. We endeavor to see where God leads. We follow in the community of faith. There is a direction about our meditation. We seek the vision of God and the vitality of community. Both inform the pathway we walk. With the practice and progress of each meditation, we move along the pathway together in the sharing and experience of faith and love. Each sharing is a step. Each experience is a movement. While we may stop and rest and rejoice at many junctures, we keep moving. For we seek to follow where God leads. The journey continues to unfold. We cover much of the same ground over and over, and yet we move forward. In reciting the biblical truths, visions, challenges, and promises, we are strengthened and renewed. This structural component to our journey is important, for it encourages us onward. For we recognize that our goal is growth. Herein, the structure is wedded with the substance.

The substance of our meditations is steeped in the biblical imagery of growth, vitality, energy, and purpose, as indicated in so many scriptural pieces that bespeak God's intention for human life. There is no shortage of biblical texts that help sharpen our focus on the substance of the growth that God intends for us, and that, therefore, ought to inform our undertaking of children's messages. Let us sample just a few.

"The substance of our meditations is steeped in the biblical imagery of growth, vitality, energy, and purpose."

First, we are invited to "grow in salvation" (1 Peter 2:2). As the Apostle Paul announced, "Now is the day of salvation" (2 Corinthians 6:2). With each meditation that we share, we participate in God's invitation to salvation—that experience of entering the waters of deliverance and moving toward the Promised Land. There is a labor involved in such salvation, for as the apostle Paul exhorts, we are to "work out our salvation" (Philippians 2:12) together as God's people. The Scriptures abound with the stories and promises of God's saving ways. We are called both to hearken and take heart: "O that today you would listen to God's voice!" (Psalm 95:7). "Tell of God's salvation from day to day" (Psalm 96:2). The wholistic and healing experience of God's salvation is that which we seek to rejoice in and encourage through the lessons we share and the relationships we nurture.

Second, we are encouraged to "grow in the grace and knowledge of our Lord and Savior Jesus Christ" (2 Peter 3:18). Our story centers on seeing, as Simeon did, God's salvation in the person and purpose of Jesus (Luke 2:30). God's grace brings salvation (Titus 2:11), and that salvation bears growing experiences of love, righteousness, justice, and peace for those who embrace it. These possibilities are what we seek to lift before our congregations with each children's message. Each meditation is a reminder of the manifold mercies of God, and each lesson beckons us to grow in the knowledge—that is, experience—of God's grace in Christ. Knowledge is not just acquaintance; it is responsive engagement. Amidst the rituals and routines of institutional religion, we must ever be reminded of the importance of grace and knowledge in the life of faith. In dialogue with the first-century religious leaders, who frequently failed to know God and God's grace (Matthew 9:13), Jesus underscored God's word as declared through the prophet Hosea: "For I desire steadfast love and not sacrifice, the knowledge of God rather than burnt offerings" (Hosea 6:6). And as the apostle John exhorts, "Beloved, let us love one another, because love is from God; everyone who loves is born of God and knows God" (1 John 4:7). Children's messages need both to revel in and nurture that love and knowledge.

Finally, we are encouraged to grow in love. We must ever be aware that as we grow in Christ, we grow in community and in love (Ephesians 4:15-16). Children's messages are an important part of nurturing a community where "faith is growing abundantly, and the love of everyone" for "one another is increasing" (2 Thessalonians 1:3). We know that the love of God and neighbor is the greatest commandment (Matthew 22:36-40). We are reminded that love is God's greatest gift (1 Corinthians 13:13). By such love, the disciples of Christ are identified before the world (John 13:34-35). Thus, by such love must our children's messages be shaped and shared.

The many biblical images of and invitations to love must ever inform and impel our lessons. Both the prophetic dimensions and pastoral depths of love need to be expressed in our meditations. We must, with the prophet Micah, affirm our calling: "And what does Yahweh require of you but to do justice, and to love kindness, and to walk humbly with your God?" (Micah 6:8). Our lessons must be permeated with the images of love in action, as expressed in God's call through Amos: "But let justice roll down like waters, and righteousness like an ever flowing stream" (Amos 5:24). Our admonitions to the children and congregation need to be steeped in the recital of the Apostle John's admonition: "For this is the message you have heard from the beginning, that we should love one another. . . . Let us love, not in word or speech, but in truth and action" (1 John 3:11,18). In the final analysis, it is the nurture of this love in truth and action that we seek in the meditations that we prepare and share. For in the meditations we share and the relationships we build, we seek to foster an experience of community, a sense of God's love, a commitment to social justice, and a passion for peace among all God's children.

"The many biblical images of and invitations to love must ever inform and impel our lessons. Both the prophetic dimensions and pastoral depths of love need to be expressed in our meditations."

Index of Liturgical Days, Scriptures, and Topics

Subjects Keyed to Page Number of Children's Meditations

LECTIONARY / LITURGICAL DAYS
(IN ORDER OF THE CHURCH YEAR)

SCRIPTURES (IN ALPHABETICAL ORDER)

TOPICS (IN ALPHABETICAL ORDER)

CPSIA information can be obtained at www.ICGtesting.com
Printed in the USA
BVOW05s0100240415

397514BV00001B/7/P